PENGUIN BOOKS
THE BOOK OF MAN

Osho defies categorization, reflecting everything from the individual quest for meaning to the most urgent social and political issues facing society today. His books are not written but are transcribed from recordings of extemporaneous talks given over a period of thirty-five years. Osho has been described by the *Sunday Times* in London as one of the '1000 Makers of the 20th Century' and by *Sunday Mid-Day* in India as one of the ten people—along with Gandhi, Nehru and Buddha—who have changed the destiny of India.

Osho has a stated aim of helping to create the conditions for the birth of a new kind of human being, characterized as 'Zorba the Buddha'—one whose feet are firmly on the ground, yet whose hands can touch the stars. Running like a thread through all aspects of Osho is a vision that encompasses both the timeless wisdom of the East and the highest potential of Western science and technology.

He is synonymous with a revolutionary contribution to the science of inner transformation and an approach to meditation which specifically addresses the accelerated pace of contemporary life. The unique **OSHO** Active Meditations™ are designed to allow the release of accumulated stress in the body and mind so that it is easier to be still and experience the thought-free state of meditation.

OSHO

The Book of Man

PENGUIN BOOKS

PENGUIN BOOKS
Published by the Penguin Group
Penguin Books India Pvt. Ltd, 11 Community Centre, Panchsheel Park, New
Delhi 110 017, India
Penguin Group (USA) Inc., 375 Hudson Street, New York, New York 10014,
USA
Penguin Group (Canada), 90 Eglinton Avenue East, Suite 700, Toronto,
Ontario, M4P 2Y3, Canada (a division of Pearson Penguin Canada Inc.)
Penguin Books Ltd, 80 Strand, London WC2R 0RL, England
Penguin Ireland, 25 St Stephen's Green, Dublin 2, Ireland (a division of Penguin
Books Ltd)
Penguin Group (Australia), 250 Camberwell Road, Camberwell, Victoria
3124, Australia (a division of Pearson Australia Group Pty Ltd)
Penguin Group (NZ), 67 Apollo Drive, Rosedale, North Shore 0632, New
Zealand (a division of Pearson New Zealand Ltd)
Penguin Group (South Africa) (Pty) Ltd, 24 Sturdee Avenue, Rosebank,
Johannesburg 2196, South Africa

Penguin Books Ltd, Registered Offices: 80 Strand, London WC2R 0RL,
England

First published by Penguin Books India 2002

Typeset in Sabon Roman by SÜRYA, New Delhi
Printed at DeUnique Printers, New Delhi

Contents

Preface

THE CHAPTER HEADINGS have been chosen to structure the wealth of material available from Osho on the subject of Man's Liberation. These archetypes—Adam, the Robot, the Beggar, the Lover, the Politician, the Gambler, the Creator and so on—should not be understood as fixed types of character or personality, but simply as descriptions of certain tendencies, conditionings and behaviour patterns of the personality, common to all of us.

As Osho indicates, our reality lies beyond all these theories and categories. These archetypal concepts are used to help us recognize our particular mindsets and then move beyond the mind's limitations and confinements—to go beyond the personality and discover our original face, the real and essential self.

Introduction

THE LIBERATION OF man has not happened yet. Not only woman, but man also needs a great liberation movement—liberation from the past, from the slavery of life-negating values and social conditionings which have been imposed upon mankind by all religions for thousands of years. Priests and politicians have caused a tremendous split in man. They have created a guilt-ridden man who is alienated from himself, fighting a permanent inner conflict which pervades all areas of his life—a conflict between body and soul, matter and mind, materialism and spiritualism, science and religion, man and woman, West and East . . .

Life can be lived in two ways: either as calculation—in science, technology, mathematics, economics—or as poetry—in art, music, beauty, love.

Every man, from his early childhood, is being conditioned to function and survive in this efficiency-oriented, competitive world, and he joins the ambitious struggle and race for money, success, fame, power, respectability and social status. As a small child, he learns to adopt the goals and values of his parents and teachers, priests and politicians, of all vested interests, without ever questioning them. Thus, he becomes distracted from his true nature, his original being, and loses the capacity for unmotivated joy, childlike innocence and playful creativity.

He is cut off from his creative potential, his ability to love, his laughter, his lust for life . . . The way he is brought up by society deadens his body and his senses and makes him insensitive and dead. He loses access to his innate feminine qualities of feeling, gentleness, love and intuition and becomes a head-oriented, efficient, unfeeling robot.

Society teaches man to become a 'strong man' which is synonymous with suppressing his feminine qualities of softness and receptivity, love and compassion. But every man has an 'inner woman' inside—his own unconscious or semi-conscious female part, which has been denied and suppressed for thousands of years.

Osho points to a third way of living one's life: with meditation. The first step is to recognize the transforming power of meditation and awareness in becoming whole, a mature individual. Meditation is the catalyst that sets in motion and accelerates the process of inner growth. Meditation makes us an integrated whole, creating a balance between our male and female parts. It teaches us to live and enjoy our life in its multidimensionality—in a healthy balance of body, mind and soul, of the material and the spiritual, of the outer and the inner world.

Man today is in deep crisis. In view of the threatening global crisis of our planet on the threshold of the third millennium, the question arises, 'What now, Adam?' The limits of growth have long been reached, the belief in unlimited scientific and social progress has been fundamentally shattered. All outer revolutions have failed. The time has come for an inner revolution.

Unless the individual man starts to come out of his robot-like, mechanical functioning and unawareness and begins to live his life with self-love, awareness, and deep respect for his real nature, there seems to be no chance that our world can escape global suicide.

'Man needs a new psychology to understand himself,' says Osho, and the basic understanding that needs to be deeply imbibed and experienced is that 'No man is just man and no woman is just woman; each man is both man and woman, and so is each woman—woman and man. Adam has Eve in him, and Eve has Adam in her. In fact, nobody is just Adam and nobody is just Eve: we are Adam-Eves. This is one of the greatest insights ever attained.'

But because man has been conditioned to deny and reject his feminine qualities, he has been trained to suppress his female part inside, which has been reflected by the suppression of the female element in the outer world. Unless man starts discovering his own inner woman, he is going to be tied up in a frustrating search for the female qualities, which are inherent in his nature, on the outside, in the outer woman. He needs to reintegrate his feminine part in order to become healthy and whole, complete within himself.

'My vision of the new man is of a rebel, of a man who is in search of his original self, of his original face. A man who is ready to drop all masks, all pretensions, all hypocrisies, and show to the world what he, in reality, is. Whether he is loved or condemned, respected, honoured or dishonoured, crowned or crucified, does not matter; because to be yourself is the greatest blessing in existence. Even if you are crucified, you will be crucified fulfilled and immensely contented. A man of truth, a man of sincerity, a man who knows love and who knows compassion, and who understands that people are blind, unconscious, asleep, spiritually asleep.'

PART 1

1

Adam

ADAM WAS THE first man, not because he was the first man—there may have been many others before him, but nobody else said 'no'. So history cannot record them; they had no egos. And this is my feeling: how could Adam have been the first man? There may have been millions before him, but nobody else said 'no'. They could not become men, they could not become egos.

Adam said 'no'. Of course he suffered for saying that; he was thrown out of the garden of bliss.

Adam is man, and every man is Adam-like. Every childhood is in the Garden of Eden. Every child is as happy as the animals, as happy as the primitive, as happy as the trees. Have you watched a child running amidst the trees, on the beach?—he is not yet human. His eyes are still clear, but unconscious. He will have to come out of the Garden of Eden. That is the meaning of Adam's expulsion from the Garden of Eden—he is no longer part of the unconscious bliss. He has become conscious by eating the fruit of the tree of knowledge. He has become man.

It is not that Adam was once expelled, every Adam has to be expelled again and again. Every child has to be thrown out of god's garden; it is part of growth. The pain is that of growth. One has to lose it to gain it again, to gain it consciously. That is man's burden and his destiny, his anguish and his freedom, man's problem and man's grandeur both.

✳

Why is it that I am never quite satisfied with who I am and with what existence has given me? I am always looking for something better to do, looking for someone else to be, always wanting when the other one has more than what I have been given. Like the saying goes, 'The grass is always greener on the other side of the fence.' Why is this?

It is because you have been distracted. You have been directed where nature has not meant you to be. You are not moving towards your own potential. What others wanted you to be, you are trying to be, but it cannot be satisfying. When it is not satisfying, logic says, 'Perhaps it is not enough—have more of it.' Then you go after more; then you start looking around. And everybody is coming out with a mask which is smiling, happy looking, so everybody is deceiving everybody else. You also come with a mask, so others think you are happier. You think others are happier.

The grass looks greener on the other side of the fence—but from both sides. The people who are living on the other side of the fence, they see your grass and it looks greener. It really looks greener, thicker, better. That is the illusion that distance creates. When you come close, then you start seeing that it is not so. But people keep each other at a distance. Even friends, even lovers keep one another at a distance: too much closeness will be dangerous, they may see your reality.

And you have been misguided from the very beginning, so whatever you do, you will remain miserable. Nature has no idea of money, otherwise dollars would have been growing on trees. Nature has no idea of money; money is a pure invention of man—useful, but dangerous too. You see somebody with much money, and you think perhaps money brings joy: 'Look at that person, how joyous he seems to be,' so run after money. Somebody is healthier—run after health. Somebody is doing something else and looks very contented—follow him.

But it is always the others, and society has arranged it so that you will never think about your own potential. And the whole misery is that you are not being yourself. Just be yourself, then there is no misery, no competition and no botheration that others have more, that you don't have more.

And if you like the grass to be greener, there is no need to look at the other side of the fence; you can make the grass greener on *your* side of the fence. It is such a simple thing to make the grass greener. But you are just looking everywhere else, and all the lawns are looking so beautiful—except yours.

Man has to be rooted in his own potential, whatever it is, and nobody should give him directions, guidance. They should help him, wherever he is going, whatever he is becoming. And the world will be so contented that you cannot believe it.

I have never felt any discontent, even from my childhood, for the simple reason that I never allowed anybody to distract me from what I was doing or what I was trying to be. That helped me immensely. It was difficult, and the difficulties went on increasing, and now the whole world is against me. But it does not disturb me. I am perfectly happy, perfectly content. I can't think that

I could have been otherwise. In any other position, I would have been miserable . . . .

The world is against individuality. It is against your being just your natural self.

It wants you to be a robot, and because you have agreed to be a robot, you are in trouble. You are not a robot. That was not the intention of nature. Because you are not what you were meant to be, what you were destined to be, you are constantly looking, 'What is missing? Perhaps better furniture, better curtains, a better house, a better wife, a better job . . .' During your whole life you are rushing from one place to another. But society has distracted you right from the very beginning.

My effort is to bring you back to yourself, and you will suddenly find all that discontent has disappeared. There is no need to be more—you are enough. Everybody is enough.

✳

Why is it so difficult for me to love myself?

Every child is born with tremendous love for himself. It is society that destroys that love, it is religion that destroys that love—because if a child goes on growing in loving himself, who is going to love Jesus Christ? Who is going to love the president? Who is going to love the parents? The child's love for himself has to be distracted. He has to be conditioned so that his love is always towards an object outside himself. It makes man very poor, because when you love somebody outside yourself, whether it is God, the pope, your father, your wife, your husband, your children— whoever is the object of your love—it makes you dependent on the object. You become secondary in your own eyes, you become a beggar.

You were born an emperor, utterly contented within yourself. But your father wants you to love him, your mother wants you to love her. Everybody around you wants to become an object of your love. Nobody bothers that a man who cannot love himself cannot love anybody else either. So a very mad society is created where everybody is trying to love somebody—and they have nothing to give. Nor has the other person anything to give. Why are lovers continuously fighting, nagging, harassing each other? The simple reason is that they are not getting what they were thinking they will get. Both are beggars, both are empty.

A rightly brought up child will be allowed to grow in love towards himself so that he becomes so full of love that sharing becomes a necessity. He is so burdened with love that he wants somebody to share it. And then love never makes you dependent on anybody. You are the giver; the giver is never a beggar. And the other is also a giver. And when two emperors, masters of their hearts, meet, there is tremendous joy. Nobody is dependent on anybody else; everybody is independent and individual, well-centred in himself, well-grounded in himself. He has roots which go deep down within his being, from where the juice called love comes towards the surface and blossoms in thousands of roses.

This type of person has not been possible up to now because of your prophets, your messiahs, your incarnations of God, and all other kinds of idiots. They have destroyed you for their own glory, for their own ego. They have crushed you utterly.

You can see the logic. Either the messiah, the saviour, becomes the object of your love, and you become just shadows blindly following him; or if you are fully contented, overflowing with love and blossoming in thousands of roses, who cares to be saved?—you are already saved.

Who cares about paradise?—you are in it.

The priest will die if you learn how to love yourself, the politician will not have followers; all the vested interests in society will go bankrupt. They are all thriving on a very subtle psychological exploitation of you.

But learning to love oneself is not difficult, it is natural. If you have been able to do something which is unnatural, if you have learned how to love others without loving yourself, the other thing is very simple. You have done the almost impossible. It is only a question of understanding, a simple understanding, that 'I am to love myself; otherwise, I will miss the meaning of life. I will never grow up, I will simply grow old. I will not have any individuality. I will not be truly human, dignified, integrated.'

And, moreover, if you cannot love yourself, you cannot love anybody else in the world. So many psychological problems have arisen because you have been distracted from yourself. You are 'unworthy,' you are not what you should be; your actions have to be corrected. You have to be moulded into a certain personality.

In Japan, they have 400-year-old trees, but their height is only 6 inches. They think that it is a form of art. It is murder, sheer murder! The tree looks ancient, but is only 6 inches high. It would have been 100 feet high, reaching towards the stars. What have they done? What strategy have they used? The same strategy has been used against humanity, human beings. They put the tree in a pot which has no bottom. So whenever the tree grows its roots, they go on cutting them, because there is no bottom to the pot. The roots they go on cutting, and unless roots grow deeper, the tree cannot rise higher. It grows old, but it never grows up. Exactly the same has been done with human beings.

Your love for yourself is a basic necessity for your

growth. Hence, I teach you to be selfish—which is natural.

All your religions have been teaching you to be altruistic. Sacrifice yourself for any idiotic idea: the flag—just a rotten piece of cloth. You sacrifice yourself for the nation—which is nothing but fantasy, because the earth is not divided anywhere into nations. It is the politicians' cunningness to divide the earth on the map. You are sacrificing for the lines drawn on the maps! Die for your religion: Christianity, Hinduism, Buddhism, Mohammedanism. And they have managed it in such a way that the individual is caught. If you die for your nation, you will be called a martyr. You are simply committing suicide, and that too for a foolish reason. If you die for your religion, you will reach paradise, you will enjoy eternal blessings. They have manipulated you. But one thing is basic in that manipulation, that is, don't love yourself: hate yourself, because you are not worth anything.

Everybody is full of hate for himself. And do you think if you hate yourself, you can find someone who is going to love you? Even you are not ready to love yourself: it is impossible for anybody else to love you. You have accepted the idea that unless you follow certain rules, religious dogmas, political ideologies, you are not of any worth.

When you were born, you were not born as a Christian, as a Catholic; you were not born as a communist. Every child comes into the world as a tabula rasa, completely clean. Nothing is written on him—the *Bible*, *Koran*, *Gita*, *Das Kapital*—no, nothing is written on him. He brings no holy book with himself, he comes in utter innocence. But his innocence becomes his greatest trouble because all around him are wolves—hiding in politicians, in priests, in parents, in teachers. They all jump upon your innocence. They start writing things on you which later on you will believe is your heritage. They have destroyed your heritage.

Now it is possible for them to enslave you, to make you do anything they want. If they want you to murder innocent people . . . .

There are religious mafias, there are political mafias, and they go on exploiting you. They may be enemies to each other, but on one point, they all agree—that a man should not be allowed to love himself. That cuts his roots from his being, and then he is helpless, rootless, just a driftwood, so whatever you want to make of him, you can.

The people of the United States were killing innocent, poor people in Vietnam. What business was it of theirs? And it was not one-sided. They were sending their own, who have not tasted anything of life, to kill and to be killed in the name of democracy, in the name of America. But why should one sacrifice oneself in any name? Mohammedans and Christians have been fighting, killing each other, in the name of God. Both are struggling with one another in the same name—God. A strange world we have created!

But the strategy is very simple: destroy the person's natural love for himself. Then he is so unworthy in his own eyes, he is ready to do anything for a gold medal, just to feel a little worth—that he is also somebody. Do you see on your generals many coloured stripes? What kind of stupidity is this? Those stripes go on growing as the general goes on killing himself, destroying himself.

You can have all those colours on your shirts. I don't think there is any law that can prevent it, but you will look simply foolish. Those generals, they don't look foolish? They are respected, they are great heroes. And what have they done? They have murdered many people of your country, they have murdered many people of other countries. These murderers are rewarded. Have you seen any society rewarding its lovers? No, lovers are to be condemned. No society allows lovers any respect; love is anathema to society. So the first thing all these vested interests have to do is distract you from love—and they have succeeded up to now.

Millions of years . . . and man has remained a slave, feeling a deep inferiority complex in himself, unworthiness, because he is not able to fulfil all that is required of him. In fact, whatever is required is so unnatural that there is no way to fulfil it. And through your worthlessness, the messiahs go on becoming bigger and bigger, because they say, they promise that they are the saviours; they are going to save you. You cannot save yourself. They never allowed you to learn swimming. On your own, you can only be drowned.

The politicians go on giving you hope that soon there will be no poverty—and poverty goes on growing. It is not decreasing, it is increasing. In Ethiopia, thousands of people are dying every day. And you will be surprised, in America, there are half a million people who are suffering from overeating, obesity; they go on becoming fatter and fatter. In Ethiopia, people are shrinking, starving and dying. In America, people are dying from overeating, in Ethiopia, they are dying because they have nothing to eat. Do you think this world that we have created is sane?

Half of India is going to face the same fate as Ethiopia soon—and India's government is selling wheat, exporting wheat to the outside world. Their own people are going to die—not in small numbers. Fifty per cent of India is just on the borderline, any moment it can become a bigger Ethiopia. But the political leaders are selling wheat to other countries because they want nuclear plants, atomic energy, so that they can also compete in the foolish race that is going on.

All this has happened in the name of altruism. I want you to become absolutely selfish. Love yourself, be yourself.

Don't be distracted by any type of people—religious, political, social, educational. Your first responsibility is neither towards religion nor towards nation. Your first responsibility is towards yourself. And just see: if everybody is loving himself, caring about himself, his intelligence will come to its peak, his love will be overflowing. To me, the philosophy of selfishness will make him really altruistic because he will have so much to share, so much to give, that giving will become a joy to him, that sharing will be a celebration to him. Altruism can only be a by-product of self-love.

Because you don't love yourself, you feel weak—because love is nourishment, it is your strength. Naturally, how can you feel responsible? You go on throwing your accountability on somebody else's shoulders. God is responsible, fate is responsible, Adam and Eve are answerable. The serpent who seduced Eve to disobey God—that serpent is responsible. Can you see the idiocy of all this dumping your responsibility on somebody?—a serpent, perhaps millions of years ago . . . . I have tried hard to converse with a serpent, with a snake—they don't speak. In fact, they don't even hear. I discovered that serpents don't have ears; ears are not part of their physiology. And if they cannot hear, how can they speak? And how could they persuade Eve? But we have to dump our responsibility on somebody else. Adam dumps it on Eve. Eve dumps it on the serpent. The serpent—if he could speak—would dump it on God. This way we go on throwing our responsibility, without understanding that unless your are responsible for yourself, you are not truly an individual. Shirking responsibility is destructive to your individuality. But you can accept responsibility only when you have tremendous love for yourself.

I accept my responsibility, and I rejoice in it. I have

never dumped my responsibility on anybody else because that is losing freedom, that is becoming enslaved, at the mercy of others. Whatsoever I am, I am wholly and solely responsible for it. This gives me great strength. It gives me roots, centring. But the source of this responsibility is: I love myself. I have also been through the same type of mass exploitation. But from the very beginning, I made it clear that if I am going to be pushed into heaven, I will refuse it. Of my own will, I am ready to go to hell. At least I will have my independence, my choice.

My parents, my teachers, my professors struggled with me. But I said, 'One thing is certain: I cannot accept any bribery to become a slave. I would rather suffer for the entire eternity in hellfire, but I will remain myself. At least that much joy I will have—that this is my choice, nobody has forced me.'

Taken as a prisoner into paradise, do you think you can enjoy it? Going into paradise following Jesus Christ, or Moses, or Buddha, or Krishna—what kind of paradise will that be, where you are expected to be blind believers; you cannot ask a question, you cannot inquire about anything? That paradise will be worse than hell. But people have been distracted from their very source.

I want you to come back home. Respect yourself. Feel the joy and the pride that existence needs you; otherwise, you would not have been here. Rejoice that existence cannot be without you. In the first place that's why you are here: existence has given you an opportunity, a life with tremendous treasures hidden within you—of beauty, of ecstasy, of freedom.

But you are not existential! You are Christian, you are Buddhist, you are Hindu. And I want you only to believe in one thing: existence. There is no need to go to any synagogue or any church. If you cannot experience the

sky, stars, sunset, sunrise, flowers blossoming, birds
singing . . . . The whole of existence is a sermon! Not
prepared by some stupid priest—it is all over the place.

You just need to trust yourself; that is another name
for loving yourself. And when you trust and love yourself,
obviously, you have taken all the responsibility of whatever
you are, whoever you are, upon your shoulders. That gives
such a tremendous experience of being that nobody can
enslave you again.

Can you see the beauty of an individual who is capable
of standing on his own feet? And whatever happens—joy
or sorrow, life or death—the man who has loved himself
is so integrated that he will be able not only to enjoy life
but will also be able to enjoy death.

Socrates was punished by his society. People like
Socrates are bound to be punished because they are
individuals and don't allow anybody to dominate them.
He was given poison. He was lying in bed and the man
who was going to give him poison was preparing it. The
sun was setting—that was the right time. The court had
given the exact time, but the man was delaying in preparing
the poison. Socrates asked the man, 'Time is passing, the
sun is setting—what is the delay?'

The man could not believe that somebody who is
going to die is so particular about the right time for his
own death. In fact, he should have been thankful for the
delay. The man loved Socrates. He had heard him in court
and seen the beauty of the person: he alone had more
intelligence than the whole of Athens. He wanted to delay
a little more so Socrates could live a little more. But
Socrates would not allow him. He said, 'Don't be lazy. Just
bring the poison.'

The man giving poison to Socrates asked him, 'Why
are you so excited? I see such radiance on your face, I see

such enquiry in your eyes. Don't you understand?—you are going to *die*!'

Socrates said, 'That's what I want to know. Life, I have known. It was beautiful; with all its anxieties, anguishes, still it was a joy. Just to breathe is joy enough. I have lived, I have loved; I have done whatever I wanted to do, I have said whatever I wanted to say. Now I want to taste death—and the sooner the better.

'There are only two possibilities: either my soul will go on living in other forms as the Eastern mystics say—that is a great excitement, to go on that journey of the soul free from the burden of the body. The body is a cage, it has limitations. Or perhaps the materialists are right, that when your body dies, everything dies. Nobody remains afterwards. That too, is a great excitement—not to be! I know what it means to be, and the moment has come to find out what it means not to be. And when I am no more, what is the problem? Why should I be worried about it? I will not be there to worry, so why waste time now?'

This is the man who loves himself. Even the responsibility of death he has chosen—because the court had nothing against him; it was just public prejudice, the prejudice of the mediocre people who could not understand the great flights of intelligence of Socrates. But they were in the majority, and they all decided on death for Socrates.

They could not answer a single argument proposed by him. I think they could not even understand what he was saying—answering was out of the question. And he destroyed all their arguments; still, it was a city democracy— the people decided that this man is dangerous, he should be given poison.

What was his fault? His fault was that, 'He makes our youth rebellious, he makes our youth sceptical, he makes our youth strange. He creates a gap between the older generation and the younger generation. They don't listen to us anymore, they argue about everything—and it is because of this man.'

But the judges were a little better than the common people. They said to Socrates, 'We give you a few alternatives. If you leave Athens and promise never to come back again, you can save yourself from death. Or, if you want to remain in Athens, then stop speaking, go into silence. Then too we can persuade the people to let you live. Otherwise, the third alternative is: tomorrow as the sun sets, you will have to drink poison.'

What did Socrates do? He said, 'I am ready to take the poison tomorrow or today, whenever the poison is ready, but I cannot stop saying the truth. If I am alive, I will go on saying it till my last breath. And I cannot leave Athens just to save myself because then I will always feel a weakling who became afraid of death, who escaped death, who could not take the responsibility of death also. I have lived according to my own thinking, feeling, being; I want to die that way also.

'And don't feel guilty. Nobody is responsible for my death, I am responsible. I knew that it was going to happen because to talk about truth in a society which lives on lies, deceptions, illusions, is to ask for death. Don't blame these poor people who have decided my death. If anybody is responsible, I am. And I want you all to know that I lived taking responsibility for myself and I am dying taking responsibility for myself. Living, I was an individual. Dying, I am an individual. Nobody decides for me; I am decisive about myself.'

This is dignity. This is integrity. This is what a human being should be. And if the whole earth is full of people like this man, we can make this earth so beautiful, so ecstatic, so abundant in everything . . . .

But the individual is missing, so you have to take responsibility for yourself. However, you will be able to take it only if you start loving whatever you are: this is the way existence wanted you to be. If existence wanted another Jesus Christ, it would have created one. To be Christian is ugly, to be Mohammedan is ugly, to be Hindu is ugly.

Be yourself, just yourself, simply yourself. And, remember, you are taking a great risk when you declare that you are simply yourself. You don't belong to any crowd, any herd. These are all herds: Hindus, Mohammedans, Christians, Communists. You are declaring yourself an individual, knowing perfectly well that it is risky. The crowd may not forgive you at all. But it is so beautiful to take the risk, to move on the razor's edge where every step is dangerous. The more dangerously you live, the more you live. And it is possible to live, in a single moment, the whole eternity, if you are ready to live with totality, risking all and everything.

I don't want you to be a businessman, I want you to be a gambler. And when you are gambling, put everything at stake. Don't save anything for the next moment. Then whatever happens will bring great blessing to you. Even if you become a beggar, your being will be far more dignified than that of an emperor.

Man cannot fall into a worse state. But he *has* fallen; he has forgotten the laughter every child is born with; he has lost his way to health and wholeness.

The door opens right this very moment—always herenow, where life and death are continuously meeting. You have chosen death orientation because it was in the interests of those who are in power, and you have forgotten that life is passing by while you are being drowned in sadness.

Once Confucius was asked by a disciple how to be happy, how to be blissful. Confucius said, 'You are asking a strange question; these things are natural. No rose asks how to be a rose.' As far as sadness and misery are concerned, you will have enough time in your grave to be miserable to your heart's content. But while you are alive, be totally alive. Out of this totality and intensity will arise happiness, and a happy man certainly learns to dance.

We want the whole of humanity to be happy, to be dancing, and to be singing. Then this whole planet becomes mature, evolves in consciousness. A sad man, a miserable man, cannot have a very sharp consciousness; his consciousness is dim, dull, heavy, dark. Only when you laugh heartily, suddenly, like a flash, all darkness disappears.

In your laughter, you are your authentic self. In your sadness, you have covered your original face with a fake identity that society expects of you. Nobody wants you to be so happy that you start dancing in the street. Nobody wants you to have a hearty laughter; otherwise the neighbours will start knocking on your walls, '*Stop*!' Misery is okay; laughter is a disturbance. Miserable people cannot tolerate anybody who is not miserable. The only crime of people like Socrates was that they were immensely happy people, and their happiness created immense envy in the great masses who are living in misery. The masses could not tolerate such happy people; they have to be destroyed because they provoke inside you a possibility of revolt, and you are afraid of that revolt. Once a man falls in love with rebellion, he is on the right path.

2

The Victim

WHY DON'T YOU know your own self? This should be the easiest thing in the world, and it has become difficult, the most difficult. This has become almost impossible, to know oneself. What has gone wrong? You have the capacity to know. You are there, the capacity to know is there. Then what has gone wrong? Why cannot this capacity of knowing turn upon itself?

Only one thing has gone wrong, and unless you put it right, you will remain ignorant of yourself. And the thing that has gone wrong is, a split has been created in you. You have lost your integrity. Society has made you into a divided house, divided against yourself.

The strategy is simple; once understood, it can be removed. The strategy is, society has given you ideals of how you should be. And it has enforced those ideals so deeply in you that you are always interested in the ideal, 'how I should be' and you have forgotten *who you are*.

You are obsessed with the future ideal and you have forgotten the present reality.

Your eyes are focused on the distant future. Hence, they cannot turn inwards. You are constantly thinking of what to do, how to do it, how to be this. Your language has become that of shoulds and oughts, and the reality consists only of *is*. Reality knows no should, no ought.

A rose flower is a rose flower, there is no question of its being something else. And the lotus is a lotus. Neither does the rose ever try to become a lotus, nor does the lotus ever try to become a rose. Hence, they are not neurotics. They don't need the psychiatrist, they don't need any psychoanalysis. The rose is healthy because the rose simply lives its reality. And so it is with the whole existence except man. Only man has ideals and shoulds. 'You should be this and that'—then you are divided against your own *is*. Should and is are enemies.

And you cannot be anything other than you are. Let it sink deep into your heart: you can only be that which you are, never anything else. Once this truth sinks deep, that 'I can only be myself', all ideals disappear. They are discarded automatically. And when there is no ideal, reality is encountered. Then your eyes are herenow, then you are present to what you are. The division, the split, has disappeared. You are one.

This is the first step: be one with yourself. The first has become difficult because of so much conditioning, education and civilizing efforts. If you have taken the first step of just accepting yourself and loving yourself as you are, moment to moment . . . . For example, you are sad. This moment you are sad. Your whole conditioning says to you, 'You should not be sad. This is bad. You should not be sad. You have to be happy.' Now the division, now the problem. You are sad: that is the truth of this moment. And your conditioning, your mind says, 'You should not be like this, you have to be happy. Smile! What will people think of you?' Your woman may leave you if you are so sad, your friends may desert you if you are so sad, your business will be destroyed if you remain so sad. You have to laugh, you have to smile, you have at least to pretend that you are happy. If you are a doctor, your patients will not feel good if you are so sad. They want a doctor who is happy, jolly, healthy, and you are looking so sad. Smile—even if you cannot bring a real smile, bring a false smile, but smile. At least pretend, act.

This is the problem: you pretend, you act. You can manage to smile, but then you have become two. You have repressed the truth, you have become phony.

And the phony is appreciated by society. The phony becomes the saint, the phony becomes the great leader. And everybody starts following the phony. The phony is your ideal.

That's why you are unable to know yourself. How can you know yourself if you don't accept yourself? You are always repressing your being. What has to be done then? When you are sad, accept the sadness: this is you. Don't say, 'I am sad.' Don't say that sadness is something separate from you. Simply say, 'I am sadness. This moment, I am sadness.' And live your sadness in total authenticity. And you will be surprised that a miraculous door opens in your being. If you can live your sadness with no image of being happy, you become happy immediately, because the division disappears. There is no division any more. 'I am sadness' and there is no question of any ideal to be anything else. So there is no effort, no conflict. 'I am simply this', and there is relaxation.

And in that relaxation is grace, and in that relaxation is joy.

All psychological pain exists only because you are divided. Pain means division, and bliss means no-division. It will look paradoxical to you: if one is sad, accepting one's sadness, how can one become joyous? It will look paradoxical, but it is so. Try it.

And I am not saying, 'Try to be happy', I am not saying, 'Accept your sadness so that you can become happy'—I am not saying that. If that is your motivation then nothing will happen; you are still struggling. You will be watching from the corner of your eye, 'So much time has passed and I have accepted even sadness, and I am saying, "I am sadness", and joy is still not coming.' It will not come that way.

Joy is not a goal, it is a by-product. It is a natural consequence of oneness, of unity. Just be united with this sadness, for no motivation, for no particular purpose. There is no question of any purpose. This is how you are this moment, this is your truth this moment. And the next moment, you may be angry: accept that too. And the next moment you may be something else: accept that too.

Live moment to moment, with tremendous acceptance, without creating any division, and you are on the way towards self-knowledge. Drop the division: the division is the whole problem. You are against yourself. Drop all ideals which create this antagonism in you. You are the way you are: accept it with joy, with gratitude. And suddenly a harmony will be felt. The two selves in you, the ideal self and the real self, will not be there to fight any more. They will meet and merge into one.

It is not really sadness that gives you pain. It is the interpretation that sadness is wrong that gives you pain, and that becomes a psychological problem. It is not anger that is painful; it is the idea that anger is wrong that creates psychological anxiety. It is the interpretation, not the fact. The fact is always liberating.

Jesus says, 'Truth liberates.' And that is of tremendous import. Yes, truth liberates, but not *knowing* about truth. Be the truth, and it liberates. *Be* the truth, and there is liberation. You need not bring it, you need not wait for it: it happens instantly.

How to be the truth? You *are* already the truth. You are just carrying false ideals; they are creating the trouble. Drop the ideals: for a few days, be a natural being. Just like trees and animals and birds, accept your being as you are. And a great silence arises. How can it be otherwise? There is no interpretation: then sadness is beautiful, it has depth. Then anger too is beautiful; it has life and vitality. Then sex too is beautiful, because it has creativity. When there is no interpretation, all is beautiful. When all is beautiful, you are relaxed. In that relaxation, you have fallen into your own source, and that brings self-knowledge. Falling into one's own source is what is meant by Socrates' saying, '*Know thyself.*' It is not a question of knowledge, it is a question of inner transformation. And what transformation am I talking about? I am not giving any ideal that you have to be like. I am not saying that you have to transform from what you are and become somebody else. You have simply to relax into whatsoever you are, and just see.

Have you heard what I am saying? Just see the point: it is liberating. And a great harmony, a great music is heard. That music is of self-knowledge. And your life starts changing. You then have a magic key which unlocks all the locks.

✻

What is repression?

Repression is to live a life that you were not meant to live. Repression is to do things which you never wanted to do. Repression is to be the fellow that you are not. Repression is a way to destroy yourself. Repression is suicide—very slow, of course, but a very certain, slow poisoning. Expression is life; repression is suicide.

This is the Tantra message: don't live a repressed life, otherwise you live not at all. Live a life of expression, creativity, joy. Live the way existence wanted you to live; live the natural way. And don't be afraid of the priests.

Listen to your instincts, listen to your body, listen to your heart, listen to your intelligence. Depend on yourself, go wherever your spontaneity takes you, and you will never be at a loss. And going spontaneously with your natural life, one day you are bound to arrive at the doors of the divine.

Repression is a way to avoid the risk. For example, you have been taught never to be angry, and you think that a person who is never angry is bound to be very loving. You are wrong. A person who is never angry will not be able to love either. They go together, they come in the same package.

A man who really loves will sometimes be really angry. But his anger is beautiful—it is out of love. His energy is hot, and you will not feel hurt by his anger. In fact, you will feel grateful that he was angry. Have you watched it? If you love somebody and you do something, and the person is *really* angry, frankly angry, you feel grateful because he loved you so much that he can afford anger. Otherwise why? When you don't want to afford anger, you remain polite. When you don't want to afford anything—you don't want to take any risks—you go on smiling. It doesn't matter.

If your child is going to jump into the abyss, will you remain unangry? Will you not shout? Will you not be a boiling energy? Will you go on smiling? It is not possible.

When you love, you can be angry. When you love, you can afford it. If you love yourself—and that is a must in life, otherwise you will miss your life—you will never be repressive, you will be expressive of whatsoever life gives.

You will be expressing it—its joys, its sadness, its peaks, its lows, its days, its nights.

But you have been brought up to become bogus, you have been brought up in such a way as to become hypocrites. When you feel angry, you go on smiling a painted smile. When you are in a rage, you repress the rage. When you feel sexuality, you repress that. You are never true to what is within you.

It happened:
Joe and his little daughter, Midge, took a trip to an amusement park. En route, they stopped for a huge meal. At the park they came to a hotdog stand, and Midge explained, 'Daddy, I want . . .' Joe cut her short and stuffed her with popcorn.

When they came to the ice cream vendor, little Midge once more shouted, 'Daddy, I want . . .' Joe stopped her again, but this time said, 'You want, you want! I know what you want—ice cream?'

'No, Daddy', she pleaded, 'I want to vomit.'

That's what she was wanting from the very beginning. But who listens?

Repression is not listening to your nature. Repression is a trick to destroy you.

Twelve skinheads, bubbleboys, walk into a pub with their Levi jackets on and all their equipment. And they walk up to the landlord and say, 'Thirteen pints of bitter, please.'

'But there are only twelve of you.'

'Look, we want thirteen pints of bitter.'

So he gives them the beer and they all sit down. And there's a little old fellow sitting in a corner and the skinhead leader walks over to him and says, 'Here you are, dad, here's a pint of beer for you.'

The little fellow says, 'Thank you, thank you, you are generous, son.'

'It's all right, we don't mind helping cripples.'

'But I'm not a cripple.'

'You will be if you don't buy the next round.'

That's what repression is: it is a trick to cripple you. It is a trick to destroy you, it is a trick to weaken you. It is a trick to put you against yourself. It is a way of creating conflict within you, and whenever a man is in conflict with himself, of course he is very weak.

Society has played a great game—it has put everybody against himself. So you are continuously fighting within yourself. You don't have any energy to do anything else. Can't you observe it happening in you? Continuously fighting. Society has divided you into a split person: it has made you schizophrenic and it has confused you. You have become a driftwood. You don't know who you are, you don't know where you are going, you don't know what you are doing here. You don't know why you are here in the first place. It has really confused you.

And out of this confusion are born great leaders: Adolf Hitler, Mao Zedong, Joseph Stalin. And out of this confusion arises the Vatican Pope, and out of this confusion a thousand and one things arise. But *you* are destroyed.

Tantra says: Be expressive. But remember, expression does not mean irresponsibility. Tantra says: Be expressive intelligently, and no harm will happen to anybody from you. A man who cannot harm himself will never harm anybody. And a man who harms himself is a dangerous man in a way. If he is not even in love with himself, he is dangerous; he can harm anybody. In fact, he *will* harm.

When you are sad, when you are depressed, you will

create other people who are around you sad and depressed. When you are happy, you would like to create a happy society, because happiness can exist only in a happy world. If you are living joyfully, you would like everybody to be joyful—that is true religion. Out of your own joy, you bless the whole existence.

✳

I have been so conditioned as a Catholic that I see no hope for myself: can you still help me?

Catholic or Communist, Mohammedan or Maoist, Jaina or Jew, it makes no difference, it is all the same. Of course, Catholics do it more systematically than Hindus, more scientifically. They have developed a great expertise in how to condition people. But all religions are doing it more or less, all societies are doing it in their own way: everybody is conditioned.

The moment you are born, the conditioning starts, from your very first breath: it cannot be avoided. Parents will condition you, the children you play with will condition you, the neighbourhood will condition you, the school, the church, the state. And consciously not much conditioning is being done but, unconsciously, the child goes on and on accumulating it. The child learns by imitating.

So don't be worried. This is the normal situation in the world: everybody is conditioned. And everybody has to come out of the conditioning. It is difficult. It is not like undressing—it is like peeling your skin. It is hard, it is arduous, because we have become identified with our conditioning. We know ourselves only as Catholics, Communists, Hindus, Mohammedans, Christians. And the greatest fear of dropping the conditioning is the fear that you may fall into an identity crisis . . . .

It is difficult to drop the conditioning, because that is your whole past, your mind, your ego, all that you are. But if you are ready, if you are courageous, if you have guts enough to come along with me it is possible, it is not impossible . . . It has happened to so many people. Become part of this happening, don't remain a spectator. Join the dance!

My invitation is for all, my invitation is unconditional.

Whatever conditioning you have got can be dropped, because it has been forced on you from the outside—and since it has been forced on you from the outside, it can be taken away from you from the outside.

I cannot give you God, I cannot give you truth, I cannot give you your inner core, but I can take all the rubbish that has been heaped upon you. And once that rubbish is removed, God starts becoming alive in you. Once all the obstacles are removed, the spring of your life starts flowing, the innocence is regained.

Innocence regained is paradise regained; you enter again into the Garden of Eden.

The modern man is suffering from the past; the modern man is not suffering from his sins as the so-called religious preachers go on saying to you. You are suffering from the sins of centuries . . . but now things have come to a peak. Man is falling apart. Up to now, somehow, we managed to keep ourselves together, but now things have come to such a point that either man has to change totally and change his vision of life, or has to commit suicide.

If you follow the past, you are on the verge of committing a global suicide. And that's what your political leaders are trying to do: preparing atom bombs, hydrogen bombs, super hydrogen bombs—piling up bombs, one after another. They already have too many! In fact, just ten years ago, they were already capable of killing each person seven times. Ten years ago they were ready to destroy this earth seven times, although a person dies only once—you need not kill him twice, that will be unnecessary. But in case somebody survives, politicians have to take care— they plan perfectly. But that is how things were ten years ago.

Now, you will be surprised: they can destroy this earth 700 times—each single person can be killed 700 times! Now this is too much, and absolutely unnecessary. Seven is okay—there are a few cunning people who may not die. But 700 times? And still the race continues. Even poor countries are joining the race, hankering to join it— starving, but they want atom bombs. Starving! but they want more power to kill and destroy.

Just a bird's-eye view and you can see the earth is preparing for a global suicide, a total destruction, a total war. And remember again, this has nothing to do with the modern man as such. The modern man is only a victim of the whole past. And the priests go on saying that something is wrong with the modern man, and they go on praising the past.

The modern man is a by-product of the whole past! Christian, Mohammedan, Hindu, Buddhist—all kinds of cultures have contributed to this situation. They are responsible. Unless they all disappear, unless we drop this whole pathological past and start anew, living in the present, with no idea of perfection, with no ideals, with no shoulds, with no commandments, man is doomed.

3

The Slave

ONE OF THE problems that every human being has to face is the world in which he is born. His being and the intentions of the world don't go together. The world wants him to serve, to be a slave, to be used by those who are in power. And, naturally, he resents it. He wants to be himself. The world does not allow anybody to be what he is by nature supposed to be. The world tries to mould every person into a commodity: useful, efficient, obedient— never rebellious, never asserting itself, never declaring its own individuality, but always being subservient, almost like a robot. The world does not want you to be human beings, it wants you to be efficient machines. The more efficient you are, the more respectable, the more honoured. And this is what creates the problem.

No individual is born here to be a machine. It is a humiliation, a degradation; it is taking away his pride and dignity, destroying him as a spiritual being and reducing him to a mechanical entity. Hence, every child, from the very beginning, as he becomes aware of the intentions of society, of the parents, of the family, of the educational system, of the nation, of the religion—as he becomes aware, he starts closing himself. He starts becoming defensive, just out of fear, because he has to encounter a tremendous force. And he is so small and so fragile, so vulnerable, so helpless, so dependent on the same people against whom he has to protect himself.

The problem becomes more complicated because the people he has to protect himself against are the people who think that they love him. And perhaps they are not lying. Their intentions are good but their consciousness is missing; they are fast asleep. They don't know that they are being puppets in the hands of a blind force called the society, the establishment—all the vested interests are together.

The child faces a dilemma. He has to fight against those whom he loves, and he thinks they love him too. But it is strange that the people who love him don't love him as he is. They say to him, 'We will love you, we do love you, but only if you follow the way we are following, if you follow the religion we are following, if you become obedient the way we are obedient.'

If you become part of this vast mechanism, in which you are going to live your whole life . . . fighting against it is simply meaningless, you will be crushed. It is wiser just to surrender and to learn to say yes, whether you want to or not. Repress your no. In all conditions, in all situations, you are expected to be a yea-sayer. 'No' is prohibited. 'No' is the original sin. Disobedience is the original sin—and then society takes revenge with a great vengeance. This creates great fear in the child. His whole being wants to assert its potentiality. He wants to be himself because other than that he cannot see any meaning in life. Other than that, he will never be happy, joyous, fulfilled, contented. He will never feel at ease, he will always be in a split. A part, the most intrinsic part of his being, will always feel hungry, thirsty, unfulfilled, incomplete. But the forces are too big, and to fight against them is too risky.

Naturally, every child, slowly slowly, starts learning to defend himself, to protect himself. He closes all the doors of his being. He does not expose himself to anybody, he simply starts pretending. He starts being an actor. He acts according to the orders given to him. Doubts arise in him, he represses them. His nature wants to assert itself, he represses it. His intelligence wants to say, 'This is not right, what are you doing?'—he drops being intelligent. It is safer to be retarded, it is safer to be unintelligent. Anything that brings you in conflict with vested interests is dangerous. And to open yourself, even to people who are very close, is risky. That's why everybody has become closed. Nobody opens one's petals fearlessly like a flower, dancing in the wind, and in the rain, and in the sun . . . so fragile but without any fear.

We are all living with closed petals, afraid that if we open up, we will become vulnerable. So everybody is using shields of all kinds—even a thing like friendliness you have been using as a shield. It will look contradictory, because friendliness means openness to each other, sharing each other's secrets, sharing each other's hearts. Everybody is living in such contradictions. People are using friendliness as a shield, love as a shield, prayer as a shield. When they want to cry, they cannot cry; they smile because a smile functions as a shield. When they don't feel like crying, they cry, because tears can function in certain situations as a shield. Our laughter is just an exercise of the lips, and behind it we are hiding the truth—our tears.

This whole society has been created around a certain idea that is basically hypocritical. Here you have to be what others expect you to be, not what you are. That's why everything has become false, phony. Even in friendliness, you keep a distance. Only so far do you allow anybody to come close. Perhaps, if somebody is very close, he may look behind your mask. Or he may recognize that it is not your face; it is the mask, your face is behind it. Everybody in the world in which we have been living has been untrue and unauthentic.

My vision of the new man is of a rebel, of a man who is in search of his original self, of his original face. A man who is ready to drop all masks, all pretensions, all hypocrisies, and show to the world what he, in reality, is. Whether he is loved or condemned, respected, honoured or dishonoured, crowned or crucified, does not matter; because to be yourself is the greatest blessing in existence. Even if you are crucified, you will be crucified fulfilled and immensely contented.

A man of truth, a man of sincerity, a man who knows love and who knows compassion, and who understands that people are blind, unconscious, asleep, spiritually asleep . . . . What they are doing is almost in their sleep. You have been conditioned for so long, for so many years—your whole life—now unconditioning will also take a little time. You have been burdened with all kinds of false, pseudo ideas. It will take a little time to drop them, to recognize that they are false and they are pseudo. In fact, once you recognize something as false, it is not difficult to drop it. The moment you recognize the false as false, it falls by itself. The very recognition is enough. Your connection is broken, your identity is lost. And once the false disappears, the real is there in all its newness, in all its beauty, because sincerity is beauty, honesty is beauty, truthfulness is beauty. Just being yourself is being beautiful.

Your awareness, your understanding and your courage that you are determined and committed to find yourself will dissolve all false faces that have been given to you by people. They are also unconscious—your parents, your teachers—don't be angry with them. They are also victims like you. Their fathers, their teachers, their priests have corrupted their minds; and your parents and your teachers have corrupted you. You have never thought that what you were being taught by your parents—who love you— by your teachers, by your priests, could be wrong. But it has been wrong; it has created a whole wrong world. It has been wrong, every inch. And the proof is spread all over history: all the wars, all the crimes, all the rapes . . . .

Millions of people have been murdered, butchered, burned alive in the name of religion, in the name of God, in the name of freedom, in the name of democracy, in the name of communism—beautiful names. But what has happened behind those beautiful names is so ugly that one day man is going to look at history as if it were the history of insanity, not of a sane humanity.

Life has been condemned in every possible way by all religions; and when everybody is condemning life—the whole world is full of condemners—what can a small child do? He becomes impressed by all this condemnation. Just look at the story of the beginning of the world. God said to Adam and Eve, 'Don't eat from the tree of knowledge, and don't eat from the tree of life.' He had prohibited them eating from two trees. They are the most significant things in life: wisdom and life—and God denies them both. Then you can go on eating all kinds of grass and whatsoever you want. He does not say, 'Don't eat marijuana, don't drink alcohol.' No, he is not interested in that. Adam and Eve can smoke grass, that is allowed; can make wine from grapes, that is allowed. Only two things are not allowed: they should not become knowers, they should remain ignorant; and they should not live, they should go on postponing life. And because they disobeyed and ate the fruit of the tree of knowledge . . . . They could not manage to eat the second tree's fruit, they were caught. After eating the fruit of knowledge, they were speeding towards the tree of life but were prevented immediately. It is natural: anyone who has awareness, consciousness—which are the qualities of wisdom—his first thing will be to go deeper into life, to taste it as much as possible, to connect himself with its centre, to be drowned in the mystery of life.

The story does not say it, but the story is not complete. I say to you they were rushing immediately, because it is absolutely logical: after eating the fruit of knowledge, they were rushing towards the tree of life. And that's why it was so easy for God to catch hold of them; otherwise, in the Garden of Eden, there were millions of trees, where would he have found them? It would have taken an eternity to search: rather than man searching for God, God would have been still searching for man, for where he is.

But I know how things would have happened—they are not told in the story. God, coming to know that they have eaten the fruit of knowledge, must have rushed immediately to the tree of life and waited there, knowing that they must be coming. It is such simple logic, no Aristotle is needed. And certainly they were caught there. Both were rushing, naked, rejoicing, because for the first time their eyes were open. For the first time they were human beings; before this, they were only animals amongst other animals . . . and God threw them out of the Garden of Eden. Since then, man has been longing for life, more life. But the priests who represent the God that has driven you out of the Garden of Eden—the popes, the imams, the shankaracharyas, the rabbis—they all represent the same guy.

Strangely enough, nobody says that guy was your first enemy. On the contrary, they say it was the poor serpent who convinced Eve, 'You are being foolish by not eating from the tree of knowledge. God is jealous; he is afraid that if you eat from the tree of knowledge, you will become knowledge. And he is afraid that if you eat from the tree of life, you will be just like him. Then who is going to worship him? He is jealous, afraid—that's why he has prevented you.'

This serpent was humanity's first friend—but he is condemned. The friend is called the devil, and the enemy is called God. Strange are the ways of the human mind! You should *thank* the serpent. It is just because of the serpent that you have become what you have become. It is because of disobedience to God that you have attained a certain dignity, the pride of being human, a certain integrity, a certain individuality.

So instead of thanking God, change the phrase. Rather than saying, 'Thank God!' say, 'Thank the serpent!' It is just due to his courtesy . . . otherwise, why should he have bothered about you? He must have been a very compassionate fellow.

Disobedience is the foundation of a real religious man—disobedience to all priests, to all politicians, to all vested interests. Only then can you throw the conditioning away. And the moment you are no longer conditioned, you will not ask what the goal of life is. Your whole question will go through a revolution. You will ask, 'How can I live more totally? How can I drown myself utterly in life?'—because life is the goal of everything; hence, there can be no goal for life. But you are starved, and except for death, there seems to be nothing; life is slipping out of your hands and death is coming closer every moment. Your life is nothing but a slow death.

And who has done this to you?—all your 'benefactors,' the do-gooders, your prophets, your messiahs, your incarnations of God. These are the people who have changed your life into a slow death, and they have been very clever in doing it. A very simple strategy is used: they say your life is a punishment.

Christians say you are born in original sin. Now, how can you have life?—you are just a sinner. Hence, the only way to get to real life is to stop this life which is nothing but sin. Who are your saints? The people who are living at the minimum, they are your saints; the less they are living, the greater they are. All your sages are living in nightmares, and they are preaching to you to follow them. Their whole effort is to cut your life as much as possible. Life is condemned, sex is condemned, having a desire to live comfortably is condemned. To enjoy anything—food, clothes—is condemned. This is cutting your life. Piece by piece life is taken away from you.

If you look in the history of Christian monasteries, Jaina monasteries, Buddhist monasteries, Hindu monasteries, you will be simply surprised: it is unbelievable that human beings have been treated in such an inhuman way, in the name of religion! All kinds of stupidities . . . .

It helps the politician if you are less alive, because then you are less rebellious, more obedient, more conventional, more traditional—you are not a danger. It helps the priest if you are less alive for the same reasons. If you are really alive, you are a danger to everybody, everybody who tries to exploit you, everybody who is a parasite on you. You are going to fight tooth and nail. You would rather die than live like a slave, because even death for a fully alive person is not death; it is the culmination of life. Even dying, he goes on living intensely and totally. He is not afraid of death, he is not afraid of anything.

That is what makes all the vested interests afraid of the living person. They have found a very subtle strategy, and the strategy is to give you a goal for your life, that you have to become somebody.

You are already that which existence wanted you to be. You are not to become anybody.

But they go on saying you have to become Jesus Christ. Why? If Jesus Christ was not to become me, why should I become Jesus Christ? Jesus Christ should be Jesus Christ, I should be myself. But what are all the Christians doing?—trying to imitate Jesus Christ, trying in some way to become Jesus Christ. Hindus are trying to become Krishna; Buddhists are trying to become Buddha. Strange! Nobody is worrying about himself; everybody is trying to become somebody else. That cuts your life completely. Hence I say: life has no goal because life is its own goal.

Drop all goals. Drop the very idea of future.

Forget completely that there is going to be a tomorrow. Collect yourself from every dimension and direction. Be concentrated herenow, and in that single moment, you will be able to know life in its eternity.

4

The Son

ALL PARENTS HOPE, and through their hope, they destroy their children. You have to get free of your parents—just as a child has to get out of the womb of the mother one day; otherwise, the womb will become death. After nine months, the child has to come out of the womb, he has to leave the mother. Howsoever painful and howsoever empty the mother may feel, the child has to come out. Then another day in life, the child has to come out of the expectations of the parents. Only then, for the first time, he becomes a being in his own right, on his own. Then he stands on his own feet. Then he becomes really free. And if parents become alert, more understanding, they will help the children to become as free as possible and as soon as possible. They will not condition the children to be of use; they will help the children to be lovers.

A totally different world is waiting to be born, where people will be working . . . . The carpenter will be working because he loves the wood. The teacher will be teaching in school because he loves teaching. The shoemaker will go on making shoes because he loves making shoes. Right now, something very confusing is happening. The shoemaker has become a surgeon; the surgeon has become a shoemaker.

Both are angry. The carpenter has become the politician; the politician has become the carpenter. Both are angry. The whole life seems to be deep in anger. Look at people, and everybody seems to be angry. Everybody seems to be somewhere where they were not meant to be. Everybody seems to be a misfit. Everybody seems to be unfulfilled because of this concept of utility; it goes on haunting them.

I have heard one very beautiful story:

Mrs Ginsberg, having arrived in heaven, addressed the recording angel bashfully. 'Tell me,' she said, 'would it be possible to have an interview with someone who is here in heaven?'

The recording angel said, 'Certainly, assuming the person you have in mind is here in heaven.'

'Oh, she is. I'm sure of that,' said Mrs Ginsberg. 'Actually, I want to see the Virgin Mary.'

The recording angel cleared his throat. 'Ah, yes. As it happens, she is in a different section, but if you insist I will forward the request. She is a gracious lady and may wish to visit the old neighbourhood.'

The request was duly forwarded, and the Virgin was gracious indeed. It was not long at all before Mrs Ginsberg was favoured with the Virgin's presence. Mrs Ginsberg looked long at the radiant figure before her and finally said, 'Please forgive my curiosity, but I have always wanted to ask you. Tell me, how does it feel to have a son who is so wonderful that ever since his time hundreds of millions of people have worshipped him as a god?'

The Virgin replied, 'Frankly, Mrs Ginsberg, we were hoping he would be a doctor.'

Parents are always hoping—and their hope becomes poisonous. Let me tell you: love your children, but never hope through them. Love your children as much as you can and give them a feeling that they are loved for themselves and not for any other use that they can be of. Love your children tremendously and give them a feeling that they are accepted as they are. They are not to fulfil any demands. Whether they do this or that, that will not make any difference to the love that has been given to them. The love is unconditional. And then a totally new world can be created. Then people will move naturally to things that they like. People will move naturally to directions that instinctively they feel like flowing in.

Unless you are fulfilled, unless you have found something that is not just a profession but something like a vocation, a calling, you will never be able to feel happy about your parents, because they are the cause of you being in this miserable world. You cannot feel grateful, there is nothing to be grateful about. Once you are fulfilled, then you will feel tremendously grateful. And your fulfilment is possible only if you don't become a thing. Your destiny is to become a person. Your destiny is to become an intrinsic value. Your destiny is to become an end in yourself.

✳

Shouldn't we be as loving as we can?

The father insists, 'Love me—I am your father!' and the child has to pretend that he loves. There is not even any necessity for the child to love the mother. It is one of the laws of nature that the mother has a natural instinct of love for the child, but not vice versa—the child has no natural instinct to love the mother. He *needs* the mother, that's one thing, he uses the mother, that's one thing, but there is no law of nature that he should love the mother. He likes her because she is so helpful, so useful; without her, he cannot exist. So he is grateful, respectful—all these things are okay—but love is a totally different phenomenon.

Love flows downwards from the mother to the child, not backwards. And it is very simple because the child's love will flow towards his own child, it cannot go backwards—just as the Ganges goes on flowing towards the ocean, not towards the source. The mother is the source, and love flows onwards to the new generation. To turn it backwards is a forced act, unnatural, unbiological.

But the child has to pretend because the mother says, 'I am your mother—you have to love me!' And what can the child do? He can only pretend, so he becomes a politician. Every child becomes a politician from the very cradle. He starts smiling when the mother enters the room—a Jimmy Carter smile! He does not feel any joy, but he has to smile. He has to open his mouth and do some exercise of the lips—that helps him, that is a survival measure. But love is becoming false. And once you have learnt the cheaper kind of love, the plastic kind, then it is very difficult to discover the original, the real, the authentic. Then he has to love his sisters and brothers, and there is no reason really. In fact, who loves his own sister and for what? These are all ideas implanted to keep the family together. But this whole process of falsification brings you to a point where when you fall in love, that love also is false.

You have forgotten what real love is. You fall in love with the colour of the hair—now, what has that to do with love? After two days, you will not look at the colour of the hair at all. Or you fall in love with a certain shape of nose or a certain kind of eyes, but after the honeymoon, these things are just boring! And then you have to go on managing somehow, pretending, cheating. Your spontaneity has been corrupted and poisoned; otherwise, you would not fall in love with parts. But you only fall in love with parts. If somebody asks you, 'Why do you love this woman or this man?' your answer will be, 'Because she looks so beautiful,' or, 'Because of her nose, eyes, proportion of the body, this and that'—and all this is nonsense! Then this love cannot be very deep and cannot be of any value. It cannot become intimacy. It cannot have a lifelong flow; soon it will dry up—it is so superficial. It has not arisen out of the heart, it is a mind phenomenon. Maybe, she looks like an actress and that's why you like her, but liking is not love. Love is a totally different kind of phenomenon, indefinable, mysterious—so mysterious that Jesus says, 'God is love.' He makes God and love synonymous, indefinable. But that natural love is lost.

You have asked me, 'Shouldn't we be loving as much as we can?' Do you think it is a question of doing something as much as you can? It is not a question of doing. It is a phenomenon of the heart. It is a kind of transcendence of the mind and body. It is not prose, it is poetry. It is not mathematics, it is music. You cannot do it, you can only *be* it. Love is not something that you do, love is something that you are. But these shoulds are heavy on your spontaneity. Love is never a should, it cannot be commanded. You cannot force yourself to love as much as you can. That's what people are doing and that's why love is missing in the world.

✻

How to love my mother?

A mother has to be loved in a totally different way. She is not your beloved—and cannot be. If you become attached too much to your mother, you will not be able to find a beloved. And then deep down you will be angry with your mother—because it is because of her that you couldn't move to another woman. So it is part of growth that one has to move away from the parents. It is just like your being in the womb and then having to come out of it. That was leaving your mother, in a way . . . in a way, betraying her. But if inside the womb the child thinks that this will be a betrayal—'How can I leave my mother who has given birth to me?'—then he will kill himself and the mother also. He *has* to come out of the womb.

First he is joined with the mother completely; then the cord has to be cut. He starts breathing on his own—that is the beginning of growth. He becomes an individual, he starts functioning separately. But for many years, he will still remain dependent. For milk, food, shelter, love, he will depend on the mother; he is helpless. But as he becomes stronger, he will start moving further and further away. Then milk will stop, and then he will have to depend on some other food. Now he is going even further away.

Then one day he has to go to school, has to make friends. And when he becomes a young man, he falls in love with a woman and completely forgets the mother in a way, because this new woman overwhelms him, overpowers him. If it doesn't happen, something has gone wrong. If the mother tries to cling to you, she is not fulfilling her duty as a mother. It is a very delicate duty. A mother has to help you go away—that's what makes it delicate. A mother has to make you strong so that you can go away from her. That's her love. Then she is fulfilling her duty. If you cling to the mother, then too you are doing wrong. Then it is going against nature. It is as if a river starts flowing upstream . . . then everything will be topsy-turvy.

The mother is your source. If you start floating towards

the mother, you are going upstream. You have to move away. The river has to go away from the source to the ocean. But that doesn't mean that you are not in love with your mother.

So, remember, that love for the mother has to be more like respect, less like love. Love towards your mother has to be more of the quality of gratefulness, respect, deep respect. She has given you birth, she has brought you into the world. Your love has to be very, very prayerful towards her. So do whatsoever you can do to serve her. But don't make your love like the love for a beloved; otherwise you are confusing your mother with the beloved. And when goals are confused, *you* will become confused. So remember well that your destiny is to find a lover—another woman, not your mother. Then only for the first time will you become perfectly mature, because finding another woman means that now you are completely cut away from the mother; the final cord has been cut now.

That's why there is a subtle antagonism between the mother and the wife of her son; a very subtle antagonism, all over the world. It has to be so, because the mother feels somehow that this woman has taken her son away from her. And that's natural in a way. Natural, but ignorant. The mother should be happy that some other woman has been found. Now, her child is no longer a child; he has become a mature, grown-up person. She should be happy, mm?

So you can be mature only in one way—if you go away from the mother. And this is so on many levels of being. A son has some day to revolt against the father—not without respect, with deep respect. But one has to revolt. This is where one needs to be delicate: revolution is there, rebellion is there, but with deep respect. If there is no respect, that is ugly, then the rebellion is not beautiful.

Then you are missing something. Rebel, be free, but be respectful because the father, the mother, is the source.

So one has to go away from the parents. Not only away, but sometimes in many ways, against them. But that should not become anger. It should not be ugly, it should remain beautiful, respectful. If you go away, go, but touch the feet of your mother and father. Tell them that you have to go away . . . cry. But tell them that you are helpless, you *have* to go. The challenge has called you, and you have to go. One cries on leaving home. One goes on looking back again and again, with wistful eyes, nostalgia. The days that have passed were beautiful. But what to do?

If you cling to the home, you will remain crippled. You will remain juvenile. You will never become a man in your own right. So what I say to you is to go away with respect. Whenever they need, serve them, be available. But never mistake your mother for your beloved; she is your mother.

5

The Robot

WHY DO THE Sufis say that man is a machine?

Man *is* a machine, that's why. Man, as he is, is utterly unconscious. He is nothing but his habits, the sum total of his habits.

Man is a robot. Man is not yet man: unless consciousness enters into your being, you will remain a machine.

That's why the Sufis say man is a machine. It is from the Sufis that Gurdjieff introduced the idea to the West that man is a machine . . . . When Gurdjieff said for the first time that man is a machine, it shocked many people. But he was saying the truth.

It is very rarely that you are conscious. In your whole seventy years' life, if you live the ordinary so-called life, you will not know even seven moments of awareness in your entire life.

And even if you know those seven moments or less, they will be only accidental. For example, you may know a moment of awareness if somebody suddenly comes and puts a revolver on your heart. In that moment, your thinking, your habitual thinking, stops. For a moment, you become aware; because it is so dangerous, you cannot remain ordinarily asleep.

In some dangerous situation, you become aware. Otherwise, you remain fast asleep. You are perfectly skilful at doing your things mechanically.

Just stand by the side of the road and watch people, and you will be able to see that they are all walking in their sleep. All are sleepwalkers, somnambulists.

And so are you.

Two bums were arrested and charged with a murder that had been committed in the neighbourhood. The jury found them guilty and the judge sentenced them to hang by their necks until dead and God have mercy on their souls.

The two bore up pretty well until the morning of the day set for the execution arrived. As they were being prepared for the gallows, one turned to the other and said, 'Dam' me if I ain't about off my nut. I can't get my thoughts together. Why, I don't even know what the day of the week is.'

'This is a Monday,' said the other bum.

'Monday? My Gawd! What a rotten way to start the week!'

Just watch yourself. Even to the very point of death, people go on repeating old habitual patterns. Now there is going to be no week; the morning has come when they are to be hanged. But just the old habit—somebody says it is Monday, and you say, 'Monday? My God! What a rotten way to start the week!'

Man reacts. That's why the Sufis say man is a machine. Unless you start responding, unless you become responsible . . . . Reaction comes out of the past, responses come out of the present moment. Response is spontaneous, reaction is just old habit.

Just watch yourself. Your woman says something to you: then whatsoever you say—watch, ponder over it. Is it just a reaction? And you will be surprised: 99 per cent of your acts are not acts, because they are not responses, they are just mechanical. Just mechanical.

It has been happening again and again: you say the same thing and your woman reacts the same way, and then you react, and it ends in the same thing again and again. You know it, she knows it, everything is predictable.

I have heard:

'Pop,' asked a boy, 'how do wars get started?'

'Well, son,' began Pop, 'let's say America quarrelled with England . . . .'

'America's not quarrelling with England,' interrupted Mother.

'Who said she was?' said Pop, visibly irritated. 'I was merely giving the boy a hypothetical instance.'

'Ridiculous!' snorted Mother. 'You'll put all sorts of wrong ideas in his head.'

'Ridiculous, nothing!' countered Pop. 'If he listens to you, he'll never have any ideas at all in his head.'

Just as the dish-throwing stage approached, the son spoke up again, 'Thanks Mom, thanks Pop. I'll never have to ask how wars get started again.'

Just watch yourself. The things that you are doing, you have done so many times. The ways you react, you have been reacting always. In the same situation, you always do the same thing. You are feeling nervous and you take out your cigarette and you start smoking. It is a reaction; whenever you have felt nervous, you have done it.

You are a machine. It is just a built-in program in you now: you feel nervous, your hand goes into the pocket, the packet comes out. It is almost like a machine doing things. You take the cigarette out, you put the cigarette in your mouth, you light the cigarette, and this is all going on mechanically. This has been done millions of times, and you are doing it again.

And each time you do this, it is strengthened; the machine becomes more mechanical, the machine becomes more skilful. The more you do it, the less awareness is needed to do it.

This is why the Sufis say man functions as a machine. Unless you start destroying these mechanical habits . . . . For example, do something just contrary to what you have always done.

Try it. You come home, you are afraid, you are as late as ever, and the wife will be there ready to quarrel with you. And you are planning how to answer, what to say— there was too much work in the office, and this and that. And she knows all that you are planning, and she knows what you are going to say if she asks why you are late. And you know if you say that you are late because there was too much work, she is not going to believe it either. She has never believed it. She may have already checked; she may have phoned the office, she may have already inquired where you are. But, still, this is just a pattern.

Today, go home and behave totally differently. The wife asks you, 'Where have you been?' And you say, 'I was with a woman making love.' And then see what happens. She will be shocked! She will not know what to say, she will not even have any way to find words to express it. For a moment, she will be completely lost, because no reaction, no old pattern, is applicable.

Or maybe, if she has become too much of a machine, she will say, 'I don't believe you!'—just as she has never believed you. 'You must be joking!' Every day you come home . . . .

I have heard about a psychoanalyst who was telling his patient, 'Today, when you go home . . .' because he was complaining again and again, 'I am always afraid of going home. My wife looks so miserable, so sad, always in despair, that my heart starts sinking. I want to escape from home.'

The psychologist said, 'Maybe, you are the cause of it. Do something: today, take flowers and ice cream and sweets for the woman, and when she opens the door, hug her, give her a good kiss. And then immediately start helping her: clean the table and the pots and the floor. Do something absolutely new that you have never done before.'

The idea was appealing and the man tried it. He went home. The moment the wife opened the door and saw flowers and ice cream and sweets, and this beaming man who had never been laughing hugged her, she could not believe what was happening! She was in utter shock, she could not believe her eyes: maybe, this is somebody else! She had to look again.

And then when he kissed her and immediately started cleaning the table and went to the sink and started washing the pots, the woman started crying. When he came out, he asked, 'Why are you crying?'

She said, 'Have you gone mad? I always suspected one day or the other you would go mad. Now it has happened. Why don't you go and see a psychiatrist?'

Sufis have such devices. They say: act totally differently, and not only will others be surprised, *you* will be surprised. And just in small things. For example, when you are nervous, you walk fast. Don't walk fast, go very slowly and see. You will be surprised that it doesn't fit, that your whole mechanical mind immediately says, 'What are you doing? You have never done this!' And if you walk slowly, you will be surprised: nervousness disappears, because you have brought in something new.

These are the methods of *vipassana* and *zazen* (Buddhist meditation techniques). If you go deep into them, the fundamentals are the same. When you are doing *vipassana* walking, you have to walk more slowly than you have ever walked before, so slowly that it is absolutely new. The whole feeling is new, and the reactive mind cannot function. It cannot function because it has no program for it; it simply stops functioning.

That's why in *vipassana* you feel so silent watching the breath. You have always breathed but you have never watched it; this is something new. When you sit silently and just watch your breath—coming in, going out, coming in, going out—the mind feels puzzled: what are you doing? Because you have never done it. It is so new that the mind cannot supply an immediate reaction to it. Hence it falls silent.

The fundamental is the same. Whether Sufi or Buddhist or Hindu or Mohammedan is not the question. If you go deep into meditation's fundamentals then the essential thing is one: how to de-automatize you.

Gurdjieff used to do very bizarre things to his disciples. Somebody would come who had always been a vegetarian, and he would say, 'Eat meat.' Now, it is the same fundamental—this man is just a little too much of himself, a little eccentric. He would say, 'Eat meat.' Now, watch a vegetarian eating meat. The whole body wants to throw it out and he wants to vomit, and the whole mind is puzzled and disturbed and he starts perspiring, because the mind has no way to cope with it.

That's what Gurdjieff wanted to see, how you would react to a new situation. To the man who had never taken any alcohol, Gurdjieff would say, 'Drink. Drink as much as you can.'

And to the man who had been drinking alcohol, Gurdjieff would say, 'Stop for one month. Completely stop.'

He wanted to create some situation which is so new for the mind that the mind simply falls silent: it has no answer for it, no ready-made answer for it. The mind functions in a parrot-like way.

That's why Zen masters will hit the disciple sometimes. That is again the same fundamental. Now, when you go to a master, you don't expect a buddha to hit you, or do you? When you go to Buddha, you go with expectations that he will be compassionate and loving, that he will shower love and put his hand on your head. And this buddha gives you a hit—takes his staff and hits you hard on the head. Now, it is so shocking: a buddha, hitting you? For a moment, the mind stops; it has no idea what to do, it does not function.

And that non-functioning is the beginning. Sometimes a person has become enlightened just because the master did something absurd.

People have expectations, people live through expectations. They don't know that masters don't fit with any kind of expectations.

India was accustomed to Krishna and Rama and people like that. Then came Mahavira, he stood naked. You cannot think of Krishna standing naked; he was always wearing beautiful clothes, as beautiful as possible. He was one of the most beautiful persons ever; he used to wear ornaments made of gold and diamonds.

And then suddenly there is Mahavira. What did Mahavira mean by being naked? He shocked the whole country: he helped many people because of that shock.

Each master has to decide how to shock.

Now, in India they have not known a man like me for centuries. So whatsoever I do, whatsoever I say, is a shock. The whole country goes into shock; a great shiver runs through the spine of the whole country. I really enjoy it, because they cannot think . . . .

I am not here to fulfil your expectations. If I fulfil your expectations, I will never be able to transform you. I am here to destroy all your expectations, I am here to shock you. And in those shocking experiences, your mind will stop. You will not be able to figure it out: and that is the point where something new enters you.

So once in a while I say something that people think should not be said. But then who are you to decide what I should say and what I should not say? And, naturally, when something goes against their expectations, they immediately react according to their old conditionings.

Those who react according to their old conditionings miss the point. Those who don't react according to the old conditionings fall silent, get into a new space.

I am talking to my disciples: I am trying to hit them, this way and that. It is all deliberate. When I criticize Morarji Desai (Indian politician), it is not so much about Morarji Desai. It is much more about the Morarji Desai in *you*, because everybody has the politician within them. Hitting Morarji Desai, I have hit the Morarji Desai in you, the politician within you.

Everybody has the politician in them. The politician means the desire to dominate, the desire to be number one. The politician means ambition, the ambitious mind. And when I hit Morarji Desai, if you feel hit and you start thinking, 'This man cannot be a really enlightened person, otherwise why should he be hitting Morarji Desai so hard?' you are simply rationalizing. You have nothing to do with Morarji Desai: you are saving your own Morarji Desai inside, you are trying to protect your own politician.

I have nothing to do with Morarji Desai. What can I have to do with poor Morarji Desai? But I have everything to do with the politician within you.

The Sufis say man is a machine because man only reacts according to programs that have been fed to him. Start behaving responsively, and then you are not a machine. And when you are not a machine, you are a man: then the man is born.

Watch, become alert, observe, and go on dropping all the reactive patterns in you. Each moment try to respond to the reality—not according to the ready-made idea in you but according to the reality as it is there outside. Respond to the reality! Respond with your total consciousness but not with your mind.

And then when you respond spontaneously and you don't react, action is born. Action is beautiful, reaction is ugly. Only a man of awareness acts, the man of unawareness *reacts*. Action liberates. Reaction goes on creating the same chains, goes on making them thicker and harder and stronger.

Live a life of response and not of reaction.

6

The Animal

I love my husband but I hate sex, and that creates conflict. Isn't sex animalistic?

IT IS. BUT man is an animal—as much of an animal as any other. But when I say that man is an animal, I don't mean that man finishes with animality; he can be more than the animal, he can be less also. That is the glory of man, the freedom and the danger, the agony and the ecstasy. A man can be far lower than animals, and a man can be far higher than gods. Man has infinite potentiality.

A dog is a dog: he remains a dog. He is born a dog and will die a dog. A man can become a Buddha, and can become an Adolf Hitler too. So man is very open-ended on both sides—he can fall back.

Can you find any animal more dangerous than man, more mad than man? Just think of a scene: 50,000 monkeys sitting in a stadium killing small children—throwing them into a fire. What will you think about them? Thousands of children are being thrown into a fire . . . . A great fire is burning just in the middle of the stadium, and 50,000 monkeys enjoying, dancing, and children are being thrown—their own children. What will you think about these monkeys? Will you not think that the monkeys have gone mad? But this has happened in humanity. In Carthage, it happened: 50,000 men burning children. They burnt 300 children at one time as an offering to their god. Their own children!

But forget about Carthage, it is long past. What did Adolf Hitler do in this century? Of course, this is a far-advanced century, so Adolf Hitler was capable of doing greater things than Carthage. He killed millions of Jews, thousands at a time would be forced into a chamber and gassed. And hundreds of people would be looking from the outside . . . watching through one-way mirrors. What will you think about these people? What type of men? People being gassed, burnt, evaporated, and others are watching? Can you think about animals doing such a thing?

During 3,000 years, man has been through 5,000 wars—killing and killing and killing. And you call sex animalistic? Animals have never done anything more 'animalistic' than man. And you think man is not an animal?

Man *is* an animal. And the idea that man is not an animal is one of the hindrances for your growth. So when you take it for granted that you are not animals, you stop growing. The first recognition has to be this: 'I am an animal and I have to be alert and go beyond it.'

It happened:

A man wrote to a country hotel in Ireland to ask if his dog would be allowed to stay there. He received the following answer:

'Dear Sir,

I have been in the hotel business for over thirty years. Never yet have I had to call in the police to eject a disorderly dog in the small hours of the morning. No dog

ever attempted to pass off a bad cheque on me. Never has
a dog set the bedclothes alight through smoking. I have
never found a hotel towel in a dog's suitcase. Your dog is
welcome.

P.S. If he can vouch for you, you can come too!'

Animals are beautiful, whatsoever they are; they are just
innocent. Man is very cunning, very calculating, very ugly.
Man can fall lower than animals, because man can rise
higher than man, higher than gods. Man has an infinite
potentiality: he can either be the lowest or he can be
the highest. He has the whole ladder in his being, from the
first rung to the last rung.

So the first thing I would like to say to you: don't call
sex just animalistic, because sex can be just animalistic—
that is possible, but it need not be. It can rise higher, it can
become love, it can become prayer. It depends on you.

Sex in itself is nothing like a fixed entity; it is just a
possibility. You can make it as you like it, as you want it.
That is the whole message of Tantra: that sex can become
samadhi (cosmic consciousness). That is the vision of
Tantra: that sex can become *samadhi*, that through sex,
the ultimate ecstasy can enter in you. Sex can become the
bridge between you and the ultimate.

You say: '*I love my husband but I hate sex, and that
creates conflict*.'

How can you love your husband and yet hate sex?
You must be playing on words. How can you love your
husband and hate sex?

Just try to understand it. When you love a man, you
would like to hold his hand too. When you love a man,
you would like to hug him sometimes too. When you love
a man, you would not only like to hear his sound, you
would like to see his face too. When you only hear the

sound of your beloved, the beloved is far away, the sound is not enough; when you see him, you are more satisfied. When you touch him, certainly you are even more satisfied. When you taste him, you feel a greater satisfaction. What is sex? It is just a meeting of two deep energies.

You must be carrying some taboos in your mind, inhibitions.

What is sex? Just two persons meeting at the maximum point—not only holding hands, not only hugging each other's bodies, but also penetrating into each other's energy realm. Why should you hate sex? Your mind must have been conditioned by the *mahatmas*, the so-called 'religious' people who have poisoned the whole of humanity, who have poisoned your very source of growth.

Why should you hate? If you love your man, you would like to share your total being with him: there is no need to hate. And if you hate sex, what are you saying? You are simply saying that you want the man to take care of you financially, to take care of the house, to bring you a car and a fur coat. You want to use the man . . . and then call it love? And you don't want to share anything with him.

When you love, you share all. When you love, you don't have any secrets. When you love, you have the heart utterly open; you are available. When you love, you are ready to go even to hell with him if he is going to hell.

But this happens. We are an expert with words: we don't want to say that we don't love, so we make it look as if we love and we hate sex. Sex is not all love—that's true, love is more than sex—that's true; but sex is the very foundation of it. Yes, one day sex disappears, but to hate it is not the way to make it disappear. To hate it is the way to repress it. And whatsoever is repressed will come up one way or the other.

Please don't try to become a monk or a nun . . . .

Remember, sex is natural. One can go beyond it, but not through repression. And if you repress it, sooner or later you will find some other way to express it; some perversion is bound to enter—you will have to find a substitute. And substitutes are of *no* help at all; they *don't* help, they *can't* help. And once a natural problem has been turned in such a way that you have forgotten about it, and it has bubbled up somewhere else as a substitute, you can go on fighting with the substitute, but it is not going to help.

Substitutes never help; they only create perversions, obsessions.

Be natural if you want to go beyond nature some day. Be natural: that is the first requirement. I am not saying that there is nothing more than nature, there is a higher nature—that is the whole message of Tantra. But be very earthly if you really want to rise high in the sky.

Can't you see these trees? They are rooted in earth, and the better they are rooted, the higher they go. The higher they want to go, the deeper they will have to go into the earth. If a tree wants to touch the stars, the tree will have to go and touch the very hell—that's the only way.

Be rooted in your body if you want to become a soul. Be rooted in your sex if you really want to become a lover. Yes, the more energy is converted into love, the less and less need of sex will be there, but you will not hate it.

Hate is not a right relationship with anything. Hate simply shows that you are afraid. Hate simply shows that there is great fear in you. Hate simply shows that deep down, you are still attracted. If you hate sex, your energy will start moving somewhere else. Energy has to move.

If God gives you sexual energy, it becomes sacred. Anything from God is sacred and everything is from God.

And by 'God' I don't mean a certain person, I mean the whole existence.

When the cuckoo starts singing, have you ever thought about what the song is for? It is to attract a sexual partner. But nobody condemns the cuckoo as obscene. When the flowers open and send their fragrance, what do you think they are doing? They are advertising that 'I have come to flower; now butterflies, bees are invited and welcome.' But for what?—because the flower has small seeds which will go with the butterflies, with the bees. Because the same division exists in the whole existence: there are plants which are male, and there are plants which are female. The male plant has to send its seeds to the female plant, its beloved.

Have you seen the dance of a peacock? Do you think he is dancing for you? And remember one thing: the beautiful tail of rainbow colours and the dancing peacock is male. He is attracting some female. It is only in the insane humanity where the female has to attract the male.

All over nature, it is the male who attracts the female. And for that reason, all over nature, the male is more beautiful—because the female need not have any beauty; just being female is enough. But strange—man has been standing on his head continuously. It is the male who should be more beautiful so that a female is attracted towards him.

But religions have made a mess. To such an extent that if you see a rich man walking with his wife, he looks like a servant, and the wife looks nothing but an advertisement for his riches. All the diamonds, all the emeralds, all the rubies, all the gold—that is an advertisement for the man. He's just a businessman; having a beautiful wife is a business strategy so you can invite your customers to your house for dinner, and your wife will hypnotize them with her beauty so that you can cut their pockets! But man has become just a servant, a businessman. His riches are known through the wife—his riches, his beauty, his genius has to be kept hidden.

Whenever you disturb nature and start manufacturing your own rules, remember it is a crime—unforgivable.

Man, unless he meditates, will go crazy—crazy after women. And man finds meditation more difficult than the woman. Experienced mothers who have given two, three births can be asked before the birth and can say whether there is a girl or a boy in their womb, because a girl remains silent, and a boy starts playing football. He starts kicking here and there.

In meditation, girls can enter deeper. On the one hand, they can go deeper in meditation; on the other, their sexuality is negative, it is not a compulsion on them.

I was amazed in my experience moving amongst all kinds of monks and nuns, because no monk is really celibate, but nuns are celibate. They can manage to be so because they don't have an aggressive sex and, moreover, nature has provided that every month their sex energy goes out of their body automatically, they are clean again for one month.

But man is in a difficulty. His sex energy can be subdued only by deeper meditation. Then he will not go crazy.

Unless you meditate deeply, you will not be able to transcend your sexual craziness.

The student demonstration had turned into a riot. Suddenly, a man staggered out of the crowd carrying a limp girl in his arms.

'Here,' shouted a cop running up to the man, 'give her to me. I will get her out of this.'

'The hell with you,' replied the man, 'go and find one of your own!'

Even in a riot, when people are being killed, shot, the man's mind remains continuously thinking of sex.

Sex is man's greatest bondage.

You have to make every effort for meditativeness, so that all your sexual energy, instead of moving downwards, starts moving upwards. Instead of finding a beautiful woman, start creating a beautiful man within you. Rather than finding a graceful woman, your energy can make you graceful.

But man is more stupid than woman. The whole of history has been made up by man, and you can see the madness: it is a history not of mankind, but of madness, wars, rape, burning living people, destruction . . . .

A married couple took their little boy to the circus. During the gorilla act, the husband had to go to the bathroom, and while he was gone, the little boy nudged his mother and said, 'What is that long thing hanging down between the gorilla's legs?'

His mother was very embarrassed and said quickly, 'Oh, that's nothing, dear.'

When the husband returned, the wife went off to buy some popcorn, and while she was gone, the little boy nudged his father and said, 'Daddy, what is that big thing hanging down between the gorilla's legs?'

The father smiled and said, 'That son, is his penis.'

The little boy looked puzzled for a moment and then said, 'Then why did mummy just say it was nothing?'

'Son,' said his father proudly, 'I have spoiled that woman.'

7

The Sex Maniac

SEX IS A subtle subject, delicate, because centuries of exploitation, corruption, perverted ideas, conditioning, are associated with the word 'sex'. The word is very loaded. It is one of the most loaded words in existence. You say 'God'; it seems empty. You say 'sex'; it seems too loaded. A thousand and one things arise in the mind: fear, perversion, attraction, a tremendous desire, and a tremendous anti-desire also. They all arise together. Sex— the very word creates confusion, a chaos. It is as if somebody has thrown a rock in a silent pool; millions of ripples arise—just the word 'sex'! Humanity has lived under very wrong ideas . . . .

Have you watched that at a certain age, sex becomes important? Not that you make it important. It is not something that you make happen; it happens. At the age of fourteen, somewhere near there, suddenly the energy is flooded with sex. It happens as if the floodgates have been opened in you. Subtle sources of energy which were not yet open have become open, and your whole energy becomes sexual, coloured with sex. You think sex, you sing sex, you walk sex—everything becomes sexual. Every act is coloured. This happens; you have not done anything about it. It is natural. Transcendence is also natural. If sex is lived totally, with no condemnation, with no idea of getting rid of it, then at the age of forty-two—just as at the age of fourteen sex gets opened and the whole energy becomes sexual, at the age of forty-two or near about—those floodgates close again. And that too is as natural as sex becoming alive; it starts disappearing.

Sex is transcended not by any effort on your part. If you make any effort, that will be repressive, because it has nothing to do with you. It is inbuilt in your body, in your biology. You are born as sexual beings; nothing is wrong in it. That is the only way to be born. To be human is to be sexual. When you were conceived, your mother and your father were not praying, they were not listening to a priest's sermon. They were not in the church, they were making love. Even to think that your mother and father were making love when you were conceived seems to be difficult. They were making love; their sexual energies were meeting and merging into each other. Then you were conceived; in a deep sexual act you were conceived. The first cell was a sex cell, and then out of that cell other cells have arisen. But each cell remains sexual, basically. Your whole body is sexual, made of sex cells. Now they are millions.

Remember it: you exist as a sexual being. Once you accept it, the conflict that has been created down through the centuries dissolves. Once you accept it deeply, with no ideas in between, when sex is thought of as simply natural, you live it. You don't ask me how to transcend eating, you don't ask me how to transcend breathing—because no religion has taught you to transcend breathing, that's why. Otherwise, you would be asking, 'How to transcend breathing?' You breathe! You are a breathing animal; you are a sexual animal also. But there is a difference. Fourteen years of your life, in the beginning, are almost non-sexual, or at the most, just rudimentary sexual play which is not really sexual—just preparing, rehearsing, that's all. At the age of fourteen, suddenly the energy is ripe.

Watch . . . a child is born—immediately, within three seconds, the child has to breathe, otherwise he will die. Then breathing is to remain the whole of his life, because it has come at the first step of life. It cannot be transcended. Maybe before you die then, just three seconds before, it will stop, but not before it. Always remember: both ends of life, the beginning and end, are exactly similar, symmetrical. The child is born, he starts breathing in three seconds. When the child is old and dying, the moment he stops breathing, within three seconds he will be dead.

Sex enters at a very late stage: for fourteen years, the child has lived without sex. And if society is not too repressed and hence obsessed with sex, a child can live completely oblivious to the fact that sex, or that anything like sex, exists. The child can remain absolutely innocent. That innocence is also not possible, because people are so repressed. When repression happens, then side by side, obsession also happens.

So priests go on repressing; and there are anti-priests, Hugh Hefners and others—they go on creating more and more pornography. So, on one side, there are priests who go on repressing, and then there are others, anti-priests, who go on making sexuality more and more glamorous. They both exist together—aspects of the same coin. When churches disappear, only then *Playboy* magazines will disappear, not before it. They are partners in the business. They look enemies, but don't be deceived by that. They talk against each other, but that's how things work.

I have heard about two men who were out of business, had gone broke, so they decided on a business, a very simple business. They started journeying, touring from one town to another town. First one would enter, and in the night he would throw coal tar on people's windows and doors. After two or three days, the other would come to clean. He would say that he could clean any coal tar, or anything that had gone wrong, and he would clean the windows. In that time, the other would be doing half of the business in another town. This way, they started earning much money.

This is what is happening between the church and Hugh Hefners and people who are continuously creating pornography.

I have heard:

Pretty Miss Keneen sat in the confessional. 'Father,' she said, 'I want to confess that I let my boyfriend kiss me.'

'Is that all you did?' asked the priest, very interested. 'Well, no. I let him put his hand on my leg too.'

'And then what?' 'And then I let him pull down my panties.'

'And then, and then . . .?' 'And then my mother walked into the room.'

'Oh shit,' sighed the priest.

It is together; they are partners in a conspiracy. Whenever you are too repressed, you start finding a perverse interest. A perverted interest is the problem, not sex. Now this priest is neurotic. Sex is not the problem, but this man is in trouble.

Sisters Margaret Alice and Francis Catherine were out walking along a side street. Suddenly, they were grabbed by two men, dragged into a dark alley, and raped.

'Father, forgive them,' said Sister Margaret Alice, 'for

they know not what they do.'

'Shut up!' cried Sister Catherine, 'this one does.'

This is bound to be so. So never carry a single idea against sex in your mind, otherwise you will never be able to transcend it. People who transcend sex are people who accept it very naturally. It is difficult, I know, because you are born in a society which is neurotic about sex. Either this way or that, but it is neurotic all the same. It is very difficult to get out of this neurosis, but if you are a little alert, you can get out of it. So the real thing is not how to transcend sex, but how to transcend this perverted ideology of society: this fear of sex, this repression of sex, this obsession with sex.

Sex is beautiful. Sex in itself is a natural rhythmic phenomenon. It happens when the child is ready to be conceived, and it is good that it happens—otherwise life would not exist. Life exists through sex; sex is its medium. If you understand life, if you love life, you will know sex is sacred, holy. Then you live it, then you delight in it; and as naturally as it has come it goes, on its own accord. By the age of forty-two, or somewhere near there, sex starts disappearing as naturally as it had come into being. But it doesn't happen that way.

You will be surprised when I say near about forty-two. You know people who are seventy, eighty, and yet they have not gone beyond. You know 'dirty old people'. They are victims of society. Because they could not be natural, it is a hangover—because they repressed when they should have enjoyed and delighted. In those moments of delight, they were not totally in it. They were not orgasmic, they were half-hearted. So whenever you are half-hearted in anything, it lingers longer . . . .

This is my understanding: that people, if they have

lived rightly, lovingly, naturally, then by the forty-second year, they start transcending sex. If they have not lived naturally and have been fighting with sex, then forty-two becomes their most dangerous time—because by the time they are forty-two, their energies are declining. When you are young, you can repress something because you are very energetic. Look at the irony of the fact: a young man can repress sexuality very easily because he has the energy to do so. He can just put it down and sit upon it. When the energies are going, declining, then sex will assert itself and you will not be able to control it.

I have heard an anecdote:

Stein, aged sixty-five, visited the office of his son, Dr Stein, and asked for something that would increase his sexual potential. The M.D. gave his father a shot, and then refused to accept a fee. Nevertheless, Stein insisted on giving him $10.

A week later Stein was back for another injection, and this time handed his son $20. 'But Pop, shots are only $10.'

'Take it!' said Stein. 'The extra ten is from Momma.'

That will continue . . . so before you become a poppa or a momma, please be finished with it. Don't wait for old age, because then things go ugly. Then everything goes out of season.

❋

Why am I so fascinated by pornography?

Must be your religious upbringing, Sunday school; otherwise, there is no need to be interested in pornography. When you are against the real, you start imagining. The day religious upbringing disappears from earth, pornography will die. It cannot die before it. This looks very paradoxical. Magazines like *Playboy* exist only with the support of the Vatican. Without the Pope, there will be no *Playboy* magazine; it cannot exist. It will not have any reason to exist. The priest is behind it.

Why should you be interested in pornography when alive people are here? And it is so beautiful to look at alive people. You don't become interested in the picture of a naked tree, do you? because all trees are naked! Just do one thing: cover all the trees, and sooner or later you will find magazines circulating underground—naked trees! And people will be reading them, putting them inside their Bibles and looking at them and enjoying. Try it and you will see.

Pornography can disappear only when people accept their nudity naturally. You don't want to see cats and dogs and lions and tigers naked in pictures—they *are* naked! In fact, when a dog passes you, you don't even recognize the fact; you don't take note of it that he is naked. There are a few ladies in England, I have heard, who cover their dogs with clothes. They are afraid—the nudity of the dog may disturb some religious, spiritual soul. I have heard, Bertrand Russell has written in his autobiography that in his childhood days those were the days, Victorian days—that even the legs of the chairs were covered, because they are *legs*.

Let man be natural and pornography disappears. Let people be nude . . . not that they have to sit nude in their offices; there is no need to go that far. But on the beaches, on the rivers, or when they are at ease, relaxing in their homes, resting under the sun in their gardens, they should be nude! Let children play around nude, around their nude mother and father. Pornography will disappear! Who will look at the *Playboy* magazine? For what? Something is being deprived, some natural curiosity is being deprived, hence pornography . . . .

Get rid of the priest within you, say goodbye. And then suddenly you will see that pornography has disappeared. Kill the priest in your unconscious and you will see a great change happening in your being. You will be more together.

A travelling salesman, staying overnight in a hotel, found a Bible by his bed. On the front page was this inscription, 'If you are sick, read page forty-two. If you are worried about your family, read page sixty-eight. If you are lonely, read page ninety-two.'

He was lonely, so he opened page ninety-two and read it. When he had finished, he noticed on the bottom of the page the handwritten words, 'If you are still lonely, call 62485 and ask for Gloria.'

✳

When you speak to us, enlightenment and bliss seem to be so close, buddhahood just a step away. So why do I behave like a grumpy gorilla when I am with my girlfriend?

Being with a girlfriend, everybody behaves like a gorilla. Otherwise, the girlfriends feel very frustrated. The more you behave like a gorilla, the more they feel satisfied. Just watch: your behaving like a gorilla is such a joy, no girlfriend is going to miss it. If you behave very gentlemanly, the girlfriend is going to be very frustrated.

But enlightenment is still one step away from the gorilla. It makes no difference where you are, enlightenment is always at a constant distance of one step. Just get out of the gorilla and you are enlightened. Sometimes it is easier to get out of the gorilla—because who wants to be a gorilla? It is more difficult if you are President Ronald Reagan or a prime minister of a country or the richest man in the world. It is more difficult for you to get out of that role—these are all roles played on the stage of life's drama.

Enlightenment becomes easier when you are playing a role which you don't like. You hate it from your very guts, but because of the girlfriend, you have to play the role. The girlfriend is also trying to play her role, but two gorillas in one bed will be very difficult to contain so man has managed that the girl should be ladylike, with closed eyes, lying almost dead, so he can jump like a gorilla all over the bed.

But you don't like the role. It would be good for you to have a camera fixed up to film you when you behave like a gorilla. And later on, seeing it, you will feel so ashamed: what are you doing? What kind of an idiot are you? It is good that people put the light off. And every society in the past has been against people making love in the open, on the beach or in the park. Every society in the past has been very much against it, for the simple reason that anybody behaving like a gorilla on the sea beach reminds every man on the beach that, 'This is what I am also doing, it is just that I do it in the darkness of the night.'

But the step from being a gorilla to enlightenment is just a single step of becoming aware of what you are doing, and slipping out of your act just the way a snake slips out of its old skin. Jump out of the bed and become a buddha. Tonight, try it! Just in the middle of being a gorilla, immediately jump out of the bed, sit in a lotus posture and become a buddha! And I promise you, your girlfriend will be even more blissful and more happy, 'At last, some sense has happened to you.'

And you will find it a surprising fact that the distance is so close. You can become in your sleep a gorilla, you can become in your sleep a president, you can become in your sleep the richest man—but these are all dreams. In fact, when you become a gorilla in your sleep, it becomes a nightmare. All love affairs turn into nightmares. And to get up from the nightmare also seems very difficult, but people only try to get up when their dreams start turning into nightmares. If the dream goes on, sweet, beautiful—who wants to get up?

It is good that you have recognized one thing—that you behave like a gorilla. This is a great understanding. Now, tonight, take the first step of becoming enlightened; and tomorrow morning everybody will see that this man—who used to be a gorilla—has become enlightened. Miracles still happen.

✳

What's the difference between normal sex and Tantric sex?

Your sex act and the Tantric sex act are basically different. Your sex act is to relieve; it is just like releasing a good sneeze. The energy is thrown out and you are unburdened. It is destructive, it is not creative. It is good, therapeutic. It helps you to be relaxed, but nothing more.

The Tantric sex act is, basically, diametrically opposite and different. It is not to relieve, it is not to throw energy out. It is to remain in the act without ejaculation, without throwing energy out; to remain in the act merged—just at the beginning part of the act, not the end part. This changes the quality, the complete quality is different then.

Try to understand two things. There are two types of climaxes, two types of orgasm. One type of orgasm is known. You reach a peak of excitement, then you cannot go further: the end has come. The excitement reaches to a point where it becomes non-voluntary. The energy jumps into you and goes out. You are relieved of it, unburdened. The load is thrown; you can relax and sleep.

You are using it like a tranquilizer. It is a natural tranquilizer: a good sleep will follow—if your mind is not burdened by religion. Otherwise, even the tranquilizer is destroyed. If your mind is not burdened by religion, only then can sex be a tranquilizing thing. If you feel guilt, even your sleep will be disturbed. You will feel depression, you will start condemning yourself and will begin to take oaths that now you won't indulge anymore. Then your sleep will become a nightmare afterwards. If you are a natural being not too burdened by religion and morality, only then can sex be used as a tranquilizer.

This is one type of orgasm—coming to the peak of excitement. Tantra is centred on another type of orgasm. If we call the first kind a peak orgasm, you can call the Tantric orgasm a valley orgasm. In it, you are not coming to the peak of excitement but to the very deepest valley of relaxation. Excitement has to be used for both in the beginning. That is why I say that in the beginning, they are the same, but the ends are totally different.

Excitement has to be used for both: either you are going towards the peak of excitement or to the valley of relaxation. For the first, excitement has to be intense— more and more intense. You have to grow in it, you have to help it to grow towards the peak. In the second, excitement is just a beginning. And once the man has entered, both lover and beloved can relax. No movement is needed. They can relax in a loving embrace. When the man feels or the woman feels that the erection is going to be lost, only then is a little movement and excitement required. But then again relax. You can prolong this deep embrace for hours with no ejaculation, and then both can fall into deep sleep together. This—*this*—is a valley orgasm. Both are relaxed, and they meet as two relaxed beings.

In the ordinary sexual orgasm, you meet as two excited beings—tense, full of excitement, trying to unburden yourselves. The ordinary sexual orgasm looks like madness; the Tantric orgasm is a deep, relaxing meditation.

You may not be aware of it, but this is a fact of biology, of bio-energy, that man and woman are opposite forces. Negative-positive, *yin-yang*, or whatsoever you call them, they are challenging to each other. And when they both meet in a deep relaxation, they revitalize each other. They both revitalize each other, they both become generators, they both feel livelier, they both become radiant with new energy, and nothing is lost. Just by meeting the opposite pole, energy is renewed.

The Tantric love act can be done as much as you like. The ordinary sex act cannot be done as much as you want because you are losing energy in it, and your body will have to wait to regain it. And when you regain it, you would only lose it again. This looks absurd. The whole life is spent in gaining and losing, regaining and losing: it is just like an obsession.

The second thing to be remembered: you may or may not have observed that when you look at animals, you can never see them enjoying sex. In intercourse, they are not enjoying themselves. Look at baboons, monkeys, dogs or any kind of animals. In their sex act, you cannot see that they are feeling blissful or enjoying it—you cannot! It seems to be just a mechanical act, a natural force pushing them towards it. If you have seen monkeys in intercourse, after the intercourse, they will separate. Look at their faces: there is no ecstasy in them, it is as if nothing has happened. When the energy forces itself, when the energy is too much, they throw it.

The ordinary sex act is just like this, but moralists have been saying quite the contrary. They say, 'Do not indulge, do not "enjoy".' They say, 'This is as animals do.' This is wrong! Animals never enjoy; only man can enjoy. And the deeper you can enjoy, the higher is the kind of humanity that is born. And if your sex act can become meditative, ecstatic, the highest is touched. But, remember, Tantra: it is a valley orgasm, it is not a peak experience. It is a valley experience!

In the West, Abraham Maslow has made this term *peak experience* very famous. You go into excitement towards the peak, and then you fall. That is why, after every sex act, you feel a fall. And it is natural: you are falling from a peak. You will never feel that after a Tantric sex experience. Then you are not falling. You cannot fall any further because you have been in the valley. Rather, you are rising.

When you come back after a Tantric sex act, you have risen, not fallen. You feel filled with energy, more vital, more alive, radiant. And that ecstasy will last for hours, even for days. It depends on how deeply you were in it. If you move into it, sooner or later, you will realize that ejaculation is wastage of energy. No need of it—unless you need children. And with a Tantric sex experience, you will feel a deep relaxation the whole day. One Tantric sex experience, and even for days you will feel relaxed—at ease, at home, non-violent, non-angry, non-depressed. And this type of person is never a danger to others. If he can, he will help others to be happy. If he cannot, at least he will not make anyone unhappy.

Only Tantra can create a new man, and this man who can know timelessness, egolessness and deep non-duality with existence will grow.

8

The Monk

ALL THE RELIGIONS have been teaching that you renounce your wife, you renounce your children, you renounce the world, you renounce comforts, you renounce everything that makes your life a joy. Then only can you be saved. They are teaching you suicide; it is not religion. But they have turned millions of people into a gang of suicidal people.

The moment your love dies, many other things also die in you. A man whose love is dead is incapable of seeing beauty in a painting. If he cannot see beauty in a human face; if he cannot see beauty in the ultimate expression of existence, what can he see on a canvas? Just a few colours. He cannot see beauty in it.

He whose love is dead cannot compose poetry, because without love, his poetry will be simply juiceless. It won't have life in it. It will be a simple gymnastics of words without any spirit behind it. It will be a corpse of poetry, but not poetry. A man who cannot love cannot be creative in any sense . . . .

The so-called celibate saints and monks have not contributed anything to human wisdom, intelligence, beauty, richness, music, dance. No, not in any dimension have your celibate monks and nuns been contributors. They have been a burden on earth.

The only thing they have contributed is Aids. And it is a very natural consequence.

Life arises out of sex, life consists of sex. You can grow your sex to such a refinement that it can become love, it can become compassion. But if you block the very energy of sex by celibacy, you have destroyed all possibilities of your growth. You are now moving towards death. If sex is life, then celibacy is death. This is a simple logic . . . . These celibates have given Aids to you, because celibacy is unnatural, against biology, against physiology, against your hormones.

And remember perfectly well that your body is autonomous. It does not work on your orders; it has its own program and it works accordingly. You eat food. It depends on you what you eat, but once it is below your throat, it is beyond your capacity to do anything about it. Now it is in the power of your body to digest it, to separate it into different elements, to send those different elements to various parts of the body: what is needed for the brain will be carried to the brain; what is needed for your genitalia will be carried to your genitalia.

And your body does not know that you are a Christian monk, that you are celibate—it goes on creating male sperm in you. What are you going to do with those sperm? You cannot keep on containing them within you, because there is only a small space; once it is full, they have to be released. And they are in a hurry to be released, because they want to go into the world and see what is happening outside. That's how you have come into the world, that's how everybody else has come into the world.

It is good that Gautam Buddha's father was not a monk. Just a few people: Gautam Buddha's father, Lao

Tzu's father, Chuang Tzu's father, Moses' father—if all these people had been monks, there would have been no religions, except Christianity—because the poor father of Jesus had nothing to do with Jesus' birth—he was a monk!

But have you ever thought about it, that the Christian God is a trinity, and that one part of the Christian trinity is the Holy Ghost. He is not a celibate, he is a rapist. A great divine act!—he rapes a poor carpenter's virgin wife, and you still go on calling this monster the Holy Ghost. Then what do you think an unholy ghost is? And he is an essential part of God. That makes God also a non-celibate.

But your monks, your nuns, all religions have forced death and destructiveness on humanity. And the ultimate result is Aids . . . . And Aids is spreading fast, like wildfire. It may destroy humanity.

Why have religions been life-negative in the past?

In the name of religion, man has been exploited—exploited by the priest and the politician. And the priest and the politician have been in deep conspiracy against man. The only way to exploit man is to make him afraid. Once a man is full of fear, he is ready to submit. Once a man is trembling inside, he loses trust in himself. Then he is ready to believe in any stupid nonsense. You cannot make a man believe in nonsense if he has self-trust.

Remember, that's how man has been exploited down the ages. This is the very trade secret of the so-called religions: make man afraid, make him feel unworthy, make him feel guilty, make him feel that he is just on the verge of hell.

How can one make man so afraid? The only way is: condemn life, condemn whatsoever is natural. Condemn sex because it is the fundamental of life; condemn food because that is the second fundamental of life; condemn relationship, family, friendship, because that is the third fundamental of life—and go on condemning.

Whatsoever is natural to man, condemn it, say it is wrong, 'If you do it, you will suffer for it. If you don't do it, you will be rewarded. Hell is going to descend on you if you go on living naturally'—that is the message of the whole past—'and heaven will be given to you if you go against life.'

That means if you are suicidal, only then will God accept you. If you slowly, slowly commit suicide of the senses, of the body, of the mind, of the heart, and go on destroying yourself, the more you succeed in destroying yourself, the more you will become beloved to God. This has been the whole teaching of religions in the past. It has contaminated man's being, poisoned him. These poisoners have exploited man tremendously out of it.

These religions of the past were death-oriented, not life-oriented.

What I am heralding is a life-oriented vision: love life in its multidimensionality because that is the only way to reach closer and closer to the ultimate truth. The ultimate truth is not far away; it is hidden in the immediate. The immediate is the ultimate, the immanent is the transcendent. God is not there but here. God is not that but this. And you are not unworthy, and you are not a sinner.

I am here to help you unburden all your guilt feelings. I am here to help you to start trusting yourself again. Once you start trusting your own being, no politician, no priest can exploit you. Man is always exploited through fear.

I have heard:

Once Mulla Nasruddin got lost in a jungle. The whole day he tried to find a way out, but he could not—tired, hungry, exhausted, bleeding, his clothes torn apart because the jungle was really thick and thorny. And it was getting darker, the sun was setting and the night was just about to come.

He's an atheist, a confirmed atheist who had never prayed. But with the situation—fear of the night and wild animals—for the first time in his life, he thought of God. He forgot all his arguments that he used to give against God. He knelt down on the ground and said, 'Dear Lord . . .' although he looked around, a little embarrassed, knowing perfectly well that there was nobody, but still embarrassed—the whole life's philosophy of atheism! But when fear knocks on doors and when death is so close by, who bothers about logic, philosophies, isms? Who bothers about reason, argument?

'Dear Lord,' he said, 'please help me get out of these woods, and I will always worship you. I will even start going to the mosque. I will follow all the rituals of Islam. I promise you! Just save me. Forgive me. I apologize for all the things that I have been saying against you. I was a fool, an utter fool. Now I know you are.'

Just at that moment, a bird passed overhead and dropped something right on his outspread hands. 'Please Lord, don't give me any of that shit. I'm really lost!'

When a man is in fear, even though he has been a lifelong atheist, he starts turning into a theist. Priests came to know about it, and then they used it down the ages. The whole past of humanity is fear ridden.

And the greatest way to create fear is to make man feel guilty about natural things. He *cannot* drop them, and he cannot enjoy them because of the fear of hell, so he is in a double bind. That double bind is the base of man's exploitation. You cannot just drop your sexuality because some stupid priest is saying that it is wrong. It has nothing to do with your idea of right and wrong; it is something natural, something in the very being. You have come out of it, each of your cells is a sexual cell. Just by saying, you cannot drop it. Yes, you can start repressing it, and by repressing, you can go on accumulating it in the unconscious, and that becomes a wound. And the more you repress, the more obsessed you become with it. And the more obsessed you become, the more guilty you feel. It is a vicious circle. Now you are caught in the trap of the priest.

And the priest himself has never believed in it, neither has the politician ever believed in it. These things were for the people, for the masses; the masses have been befooled.

The stories say that kings used to have hundreds of wives, and so was the case with priests. And it is a miracle: the people continued to believe in these charlatans . . . . The priest and the politician have both been doing all that they have been telling the people not to do, sometimes openly, sometimes from the back door . . . .

The priests have tremendously harmed the human heart, human consciousness. They have put this poisonous idea in man that life is something ugly. They have been teaching people how to get rid of life.

I teach my people how to get deeper into it. They have been teaching how to be free of life. I teach how to make your life free. They have been teaching how to end this life, and I am teaching you how to move into it for eternity, on and on, how to live life abundantly. Hence, the controversy; it is bound to be there. My vision is just the opposite to what has been taught in the name of religion.

I am bringing a new vision of religion to the world.

This is the boldest attempt ever made: to accept life in its multidimensionality, to enjoy it, to celebrate it, to rejoice in it. Renunciation is not my way, but rejoicing. Fasting is not my way, but feasting. And to be festive is to be religious. My definition of religion is the festive dimension.

No other animal can be festive; no other animal knows anything about festivals. Porpoises can play, chimpanzees can play; only man celebrates.

Celebration is the highest growth of consciousness. I teach you celebration. Celebration is my key.

9

The Homosexual

In the primal group that I have just finished, I was facing my homosexuality. The therapist said that emotionally I am like a little boy. What do you say?

THE FIRST THING: don't make it a problem. If you really want to solve it, don't make it a problem. Once you make it a problem then there is no solution to it. It will look paradoxical but what I am saying is: accept it—nothing is wrong in it. It is just a social idea that something is wrong in it, but nothing is wrong. It is good at least that you feel attracted to *some*body. So the first thing is to accept it, don't reject it; otherwise you will never be able to solve it. Through acceptance, there is a possibility of its disappearance. The more you reject it, the more you will become attracted to boys, because whatsoever is rejected creates attraction. Live it out and it will disappear.

Homosexuality is a necessary phase in the growth of a man or a woman.

(Osho goes on to explain the four stages of sexual growth, from auto-sexuality in a child, to homosexuality which naturally precedes heterosexuality, and then the last

phase of going beyond phase—brahmacharya.)

The primal therapist seems to be right: you got stuck in the second phase. Nothing is wrong in it. You can go beyond it but you can go only through it. So drop any attitude about homosexuality; that is nothing but the propaganda of the ages. Nothing is wrong in it, it is not a sin. And if you can accept it, then naturally you will grow out of it and you will start being interested in women, but you have to pass through it.

It is possible that your mother was more dominating, as mothers always are. It is very rare to find a man who is not a henpecked husband—very rare. In fact, it doesn't happen, and if sometimes you find one, then the exception proves the rule and nothing else. There are reasons, psychological reasons for it.

The man continuously fights in the world so his male energy is exhausted. By the time he comes home, he wants to become feminine. He wants to rest from his male aggression. In the office, in the factory, in the marketplace, in politics—everywhere he has been fighting and fighting. At home, he does not want to fight, he wants to rest, because tomorrow again the world will start. So the moment he enters the house, he becomes feminine. The whole day the woman has been feminine, not fighting at all; there was nobody to fight with. She is tired of being a woman . . . and the kitchen and everything and the children. She wants to enjoy a little bit of aggression and fight and nagging, and the poor husband is available. So she becomes male and the husband becomes female; that is the whole foundation of henpeckedness.

But children get into trouble: they see that the mother is dominating; they feel sorry for the father, and out of their feeling of sympathy for the father they want to love him. But they cannot—they cannot go against the mother.

Even the father cannot go against the mother, how can they? Deep down, they resist the mother; the dominating mother becomes repulsive, and that is their first experience of womanhood. Later on, whenever they are with women, they will be afraid; she is going to prove a mother again. She will dominate, she will nag, she will be powerful.

That is your fear, and you are still in sympathy with your father. The poor old man never had a say. Because of that sympathy with the father, you are more attracted to boys. But this thing is nothing to be thought of as a problem. You can go through it. Start enjoying it and don't feel guilty about it. Soon you will be surprised—a great desire for women will arise in you. Because being attracted to a man is one thing, but to be fulfilled by a man is not possible. Fulfilment needs the opposite, because the opposite complements. You may feel good with a man, but to feel good is one thing and to be in deep, intimate love is another. You may feel happy, but to feel happy is one thing and to be ecstatic is totally another.

Ecstasy is possible only when male and female energies meet, but ecstasy always brings in its shadow, agony. That's the fear: you have seen the agony too much and you are afraid. But the ecstasy is so beautiful that it is worth all the agony—the fight, the conflict. Men are better friends, remember; man and woman are never friends. Lovers are enemies but never friends; in fact, lovers and enemies, never friends. Men are very good friends; women don't know how to be friendly. It is very difficult for women to love other women; they know each other too well—in fact they know too much about each other. But men are very friendly and homosexuals are really gay people, because there is no agony . . . but there is no ecstasy either. One has to risk and pay.

My suggestion is: accept this and soon you will pass

beyond it. Then you will start exploring the opposite polarity: the woman. It has to be explored, it is part of growth. The man has to explore the woman, the woman has to explore the man. And the deeper you go into that exploration, the more ecstasy will arise, and the more possibility of agony will be there too. They go together, they balance each other.

A man-to-man relationship is more comfortable, convenient, more understanding. A man-woman relationship is always a turmoil, less understanding because they are such worlds apart. How can they understand each other? No man understands the woman, no woman understands the man, and that is the beauty of their being together. That creates mystery . . . and misunderstanding too.

But first accept it. Drop your resistance, and soon you will be able to go beyond it.

Whenever two similar types of bodies and minds try to fit into each other, this is perversion. So I say that homosexuality is a perversion.

In the West, now, it has become more and more prevalent. Now homosexuals think they are progressive: they have their clubs, parties, institutions, magazines, propaganda, everything. And their number is rising: in certain countries, it has come to near about 40 per cent. Sooner or later, homosexuality will become a pattern all over, a normal pattern. Now even certain states in America are allowing homosexual marriage. If people insist, you have to allow it because the government has to serve the people.

If two men want to live together in marriage, it is no one's business to create obstacles. It's okay. If two women want to live together, married, it's no one's business. It's their own affair. But this is basically unscientific. It is their affair, but unscientific. It is their affair and no one needs to interfere, but their minds are unenlightened about the very basic pattern of human energy and its movement.

Homosexuals cannot develop spirituality. It is very difficult. Their whole pattern of energy movement is disturbed. The whole mechanism is shocked, perverted. And now if homosexuality grows too much in the world, very different techniques will have to be developed, unknown before, to help them to move towards meditation.

After ten years in the army, the men are sent for a medical check-up. The soldiers strip off their clothes and enter the doctor's office one by one.

The doctor puts his stethoscope on the first man's chest and says, 'Sophia Loren.' The man's heart beats quickly—'Boom! Boom! Boom!'

'Raquel Welch,' says the doctor—'Boom! Boom! Boom!'

'Your wife,' says the doctor—'Boom.'

'Perfectly normal,' announces the doctor. 'Go and stand over there.'

The next man is examined in the same way. 'Marilyn Monroe,' says the doctor—'Boom! Boom! Boom!'

'Your wife'—complete silence. 'Good,' says the doctor, 'go and stand with the other men.'

The next man comes for the examination.

'Sophia Loren,' says the doctor—'Boom . . . boom . . . boom . . . .'

'Brigitte Bardot,' tries the doctor—'Boom . . . boom . . . boom . . . .'

'Your wife,' says the doctor—'. . . Boom.'

'Strange,' says the doctor, 'but still you are quite normal. Anyway, go and stand with the other men.'— 'Boom! Boom! Boom! Boom!'

10

The Zorba

HAVE YOU READ *Zorba the Greek*? Read it! Zorba says to his boss, 'There is something missing in you, boss. A touch of madness! Unless you cut the string, you will never really live.'

A little madness gives you dimension, gives you poetry, and gives you enough courage to be happy in this unhappy world.

Zorba has his own beauty. Kazantzakis, who created the novel *Zorba the Greek*, is one of the best novelists of this century, and he suffered tremendously at the hands of the church.

Zorba is a fictitious name, he is not a historical person. When Kazantzakis wrote *Zorba the Greek*, he was expelled from the church. By writing *Zorba*, he was forced, 'You withdraw your book *Zorba*; otherwise you will be expelled.' Because he did not withdraw the book, he was expelled from Christianity and condemned to hell.

Zorba is really Kazantzakis' own individuality that Christianity had repressed, which he could not live, which he wanted to live. He expressed that whole unlived part of his life in the name of Zorba. Zorba is a beautiful man— no fear of hell, no greed for heaven, living moment to moment, enjoying small things . . . food, drink, women. After the whole day's work, he will take his musical instrument and will dance on the beach for hours.

And the other part of Kazantzakis which he lived in *Zorba the Greek* . . . Zorba is the servant; the other part is the master who employed Zorba as his servant. He is always sad and sitting in his office, doing his files, never laughing, never enjoying, never going out and always feeling deep down jealous of Zorba because he earns a little, not much, but he lives like an emperor, not thinking of tomorrow, of what will happen. He eats well, he drinks well, he sings well, he dances well. And his master, who is very rich, is just sitting there sad, tense, in anguish, in misery, suffering.

Zorba is the unlived part of every so-called religious person.

And why was the church so against it when *Zorba* was published? It was just a novel; there was nothing for the church to be worried about. But it was so clear that it is the unlived Christian in every Christian, this book could be a dangerous book. And it *is* a dangerous book.

But Zorba is tremendously beautiful. Kazantzakis sends him to purchase some things from the city, and he forgets all. He drinks and goes to the prostitutes and enjoys, and once in a while, he remembers that it seems many days have passed, but still the money is with him. Unless all the money is finished, how can he return? The master will be very angry, but nothing can be done about it—it is *his* problem. After three weeks he comes back—he had gone only for three days—and he does not bring anything that he was sent for. And he comes with all the stories—'What a great journey it was, you should have been there. I met such beautiful Bubulinas . . . and such good wine!'

The master said, 'But what about the things? For three

weeks, I have been sitting here boiling.'

He said, 'When there are so many beautiful things available, who bothers about such small things? You can cut my salary every week, by and by, slowly, and take your money back. I am sorry I could not come earlier. And you should be happy that I have come. Because the money was finished I *had* to come. But next time when I go, I will bring all the things.'

He said, 'You will never go again, I will send somebody else.'

Zorba's whole life is a life of simple physical enjoyment, but without any anxiety, without any guilt, without any botheration about sin and virtue.

Nikos Kazantzakis represents you—each human being. He was a rare man, but a victim of the whole past. He was a very sensitive man; that's why the split became very clear; a very intelligent man, he could see he was divided. That created great inner torture for him.

To be divided against yourself is hell, fighting with yourself is continuous torture. You want to do something— that is one part of you—and the second part says, 'No, you cannot do it. It is sin.' How can you be at peace with yourself? And one who is not at peace with himself cannot be at peace with society, with culture and, finally, with existence. The individual is the very brick of the whole existence.

I would like this man Zorba to be alive in everybody, because it is your natural inheritance. But you should not stop at Zorba. Zorba is only the beginning.

I would like you to be Zorba the Greek and Gautam the Buddha together, simultaneously. Less than that won't do. Zorba represents the earth with all its flowers and greenery and mountains and rivers and oceans. Buddha represents the sky with all its stars and clouds, and the rainbows. The sky without the earth will be empty. The sky cannot laugh without the earth. The earth without the sky will be dead. Both together—and a dance comes into existence. The earth and the sky dancing together . . . and there is laughter, there is joy, there is celebration.

If a man can be authentically a Zorba, he is not far away from being a Buddha. He has travelled almost half the path. And the first half is the most difficult because all religions are against it. All religions drag you somewhere else, away from the first half; and once you are dragged in some other direction, you can never be a Buddha—because only this way goes to Buddha.

Zorba is the way to Buddha.

Since I met you, I started daring to love, laugh, and dance again. You opened my eyes to beauty, to the poetry of life. I feel younger, almost childlike, amazed by the beauty which permeates everything—a young pagan roving with pleasure, drinking the juice, enjoying every drop of it. Is it deeply immoral?

No, it is immensely moral. It is the only morality there is—to be a pagan, to squeeze every drop of juice of every moment in life; to be a child, innocent, again running after butterflies, collecting seashells on the beach, coloured stones . . . seeing the beauty of existence which surrounds you, allowing yourself to love and be loved. Love is the beginning of religion. And love is also the end of religion.

And a religious person is always young. Even when he is dying, he is young. Even in his death, he is full of joy, full of dance, full of song.

I teach you to be pagans and to have the innocence of children. I teach you to know the wonder and the mystery of existence—not to analyse it but to enjoy it, not to make a theory out of it but to make a dance out of it.

The whole existence is dancing, except men. They have become a big graveyard. I am calling you to come out of your graves.

No, it is not immoral. All the religions will say it is, but all those religions are wrong. Whoever says this is immoral is just against humanity, against existence, against joy, against bliss, against everything that leads to godliness. I am all for it.

PART 2

The man or the woman
Is still alone,
But a lover is formed
When the souls cojoin.

—The Baul mystics

PART X

11

Eve

Some days I feel like a man and others like a woman. Can I be both? Or will I grow up schizy?

EVERYBODY IS BOTH, and you have become aware of it. That's very good, that's a great insight into your being. Everybody is both, but up to now society has been conditioned in such a way, we have been taught and brought up in such a way that man is man, woman is woman. This is a very false arrangement, untrue to nature. If a man starts crying and weeping, people start telling him, 'Don't weep like a woman, don't cry like a woman; don't be a sissy.' This is nonsense—because a man has as many tear-glands in his eyes as a woman. If nature had not meant him to cry and weep, there would have been no tear-glands.

Now this is very repressive. If a girl starts behaving like a man, is ambitious, aggressive, people start thinking that something is wrong: something hormonal is wrong. They call her a tomboy; she is not a girl. This is nonsense! This division is not natural; this division is political, social.

Women have been forced to play the role of women twenty-four hours a day, and men have been forced to play the role of men twenty-four hours a day—which is very unnatural and certainly creates much misery in the world.

There are moments when a man is soft and should be feminine. There are moments when the husband should be the wife and the wife should be the husband, and this should be very natural. And there will be more rhythm and more harmony. If a man is not *supposed* to be a man twenty-four hours a day, he will be more relaxed. And if a woman is not supposed to be a woman twenty-four hours a day, she will be more natural and spontaneous.

Yes, sometimes in a rage, a woman becomes more dangerous than a man, and sometimes in soft moments, a man is more loving than any woman—and these moments go on changing. Both these climates are yours; so don't think that you are becoming schizophrenic or something. This duality is part of nature.

A good insight has happened to you. Don't lose it, and don't be worried that you are going schizophrenic. It is a shift: a few hours you are man, a few hours you are woman. If you watch it, you can know exactly how many minutes you are a man and how many minutes you are a woman. It is a periodical change. In yoga, they have worked hard on these inner secrets. If you watch your breath, that will give you the time exactly. When one nostril, the left nostril, is breathing, you are feminine. When the right nostril is breathing, you are male. And after nearabout forty-eight minutes, they change.

Continuously—day and night—this change happens. When you are breathing from the left nostril, your right-brain hemisphere functions: the right is the feminine part. When you are breathing from the right nostril, your left brain functions: that is the male part. And sometimes you can play games with it.

If you are very angry then do one thing: close your

right nostril and start breathing from the left, and within seconds, you will see the anger has disappeared—because to be angry, you need to be in the male part of your being. Try it and you will be surprised. Just by changing the breath from one nostril to another, something of tremendous importance changes. If you are feeling very cold towards the world, then breathe from the left nostril and let your imagination, fantasy, warmth flow in—and you will suddenly feel full of warmth.

And there are acts which can be done more easily when you are in the male climate. When you are doing something hard—carrying a rock, pushing a rock—check your nostril. If it is not in the male climate, it is not good. It may be dangerous for the body: you will be very soft. When you are playing with a child, or just sitting with your dog, feel that you are in the feminine—more affinity will arise. When you are writing a poem or painting or making music, you should be in the feminine . . . unless you are trying to create war music! Then it is okay, you should be in the male climate—aggressive.

Watch it, and you will become more and more aware of these two polarities. And this is good that these two polarities exist: that's how nature arranges for rest. When your male part becomes tired, you move to the female part; the male part rests. When the female part is tired, you rest; you become male. And this is an inner economy—one goes on changing. But your society has taught you wrong things: that a man is a man, and *has* to be a man twenty-four hours a day—this is too much of a duty. And a woman has to be a woman twenty-four hours a day—soft, loving, compassionate: this is too much of a duty. Sometimes, she also wants to fight, be angry, throw things . . . and this is good, if you understand the inner play.

These two polarities are a good inner play—the play of

consciousness. This is how God has become divided in you, to have a play of hide-and-seek with himself. When the play is over, when you have learnt that which is to be learnt from the play, when the lesson has been learnt, then you pass beyond.

The ultimate stage is neither male nor female: it is neutral.

Man is aware deep down that woman has something which he does not have. In the first place, the woman is attractive to him, she looks beautiful. He falls in love with the woman, the woman becomes almost an addiction to him—and that's where the trouble arises.

The feeling of dependence on woman, which every man feels, makes him react in such a way that he tries to manage the woman as a slave—spiritually a slave. He is also afraid because she is beautiful. She is beautiful not only to him: she is beautiful to whomever looks at her, to whomever comes in contact with her. Great jealousy arises in the egoist, male chauvinist mind. He has done with women what Machiavelli suggests to politicians—marriage is politics too. Machiavelli suggests that the best way of defence is offense, and man has used the idea for centuries— centuries before Machiavelli recognized it as a basic fact in all political spheres. Wherever there is some kind of domination, offense is certainly the best way of defence. In defence, you are already losing ground; you have already accepted yourself as the defeated side. You are just protecting yourself.

In India, there are religious scriptures like *Manu Smriti*, 5,000 years old, and they suggest that if you want to have peace in your house, giving a good beating to the woman once in a while is absolutely necessary. She should be kept almost imprisoned. And that's how she has lived—in different cultures, different countries, but her imprisonment has been almost the same. And because man wanted to prove himself superior . . . . Remember, whenever you want to prove something, that means you are not that thing. A real superiority needs no proof, no evidence, no witness, no argument. A real superiority is immediately recognized by anybody who has even a small amount of intelligence. The real superiority has its own magnetic force.

Because men condemned woman—and they had to condemn her to keep her in control—they reduced her almost to a subhuman category. What fear must have led man to do this?—because it is sheer paranoia. Man continuously compares and finds the woman superior. For example, in making love to a woman, a man is very inferior because he can have only one orgasm at a time while the woman can have at least half a dozen, a chain— multiple orgasm. Man simply feels utterly helpless. He cannot give those orgasms to the woman. And this has created one of the most miserable things in the world: because he cannot give a multiple orgasm, he has tried not to give her even the first orgasm. The taste of the orgasm can create danger for him.

If the woman knows what orgasm is, she is bound to become aware that one orgasm is not satisfying; on the contrary, she is more thirsty. But the man is spent, so the most cunning way is not to let the woman know that anything like orgasm exists in the world. And because the woman has not known orgasm, you should not think that man has been in a better position. Not giving orgasm to the woman, he has to lose his own orgasm too.

Something significant has to be understood: man's sexuality is local, it is confined to the genitals and a sex centre in the brain. But with the woman, it is different: her sexuality is all over her body. Her whole body is sensitive, is erotic. Because man's sexuality is local, it is tiny. The woman's sexuality is something very great. Man is finished within a few seconds; the woman is not even warmed up. Man is in such a hurry—as if he is doing some duty for which he is paid and wants to finish it quickly. Making love is the same.

Why, in fact, does man bother to make love, I wonder?—just two or three seconds and he is finished! The woman was warming up, and the man is finished. Not that he has attained orgasm; ejaculation is not orgasm. The man turns on his side and goes to sleep. And the woman— not one woman but millions of women are crying tears after men have made love to them because they have been left in a limbo. You have encouraged them and before they can come to a conclusion, you are out of the game.

But this fact of the man finishing quickly has a very significant background; that's what I have been bringing you to. In not allowing the woman the first orgasm, he has to learn to finish as quickly as possible. So the woman loses something tremendously beautiful, something sacred on the earth—and the man has lost it too.

Orgasm is not the only thing in which the woman is powerful. Everywhere in the world the woman lives five years longer than the man; her average age is five years more than the man's. That means she has more resistance and stamina. Women are sick less than men. Women, even if they are sick, heal themselves more quickly than men. These are scientific facts.

One hundred and fifteen boys are born while 100 girls are born. One wonders: why 115? But nature knows better. By the time they are marriageable, fifteen boys will have popped off! Only 100 boys and 100 girls will be left. Girls don't die easily. Women don't commit suicide as much as men; men's suicide rate is double theirs. Although women talk about suicide more than men—man ordinarily never talks about it . . . . Women make much fuss about suicide but they always choose to survive because they don't use any drastic methods to kill themselves. They choose the most comfortable, scientific and contemporary—sleeping pills. And, strangely enough, no woman takes so many pills that it becomes impossible for her to be revived. So her suicide is not suicide but a kind of protest, a threat, a blackmail to make the husband understand that this is a warning for the future. Everybody is condemning him—the doctors, the neighbours, the relatives, the police officers. He has unnecessarily become a criminal, and everybody's sympathy is for the woman—although she was going to commit suicide.

As far as murder is concerned, the difference is vast. Man commits murder almost twenty times more; a woman, very rarely. Women go mad less than men. Again, the proportion is the same: men go mad twice as often as women.

And still, after all these facts established by science, the superstition continues that man is stronger. Only in one thing is he stronger and that is he has a muscular body. He is a good manual worker. Otherwise, on every point he feels—and he has felt for centuries—a deep inferiority complex. To avoid that complex, the only way is to force woman into an inferior position. And that is the only thing that is more powerful in man: he can force woman. He is more cruel, he is more violent, and he has forced woman to accept an idea which is absolutely false: that she is weak. And to prove that woman is weak, he has to condemn all the feminine qualities. He has to say that they are all weak, and all those qualities together make woman weak.

In fact, woman has all the great qualities in her. And

whenever a man becomes awakened, he attains to the same qualities which he has been condemning in women. The traits that are thought to be weak are all the feminine ones. And it is a strange fact that all the great characteristics come into that category. What is left are only the brutal qualities, animal qualities.

Woman is more loving. Man has not shown greater love than woman. In India, millions of women have died—they have jumped alive into the funeral pyre with their beloveds because they could not conceive of a life without their husband or friend. But don't you think it is a little weird that in 10,000 years not a single man has dared to jump into a funeral pyre with his wife? Enough time, enough opportunity . . . and you are stronger. The delicate woman, the fragile woman, jumps into the funeral pyre and the stronger Mohammed Ali goes on doing his push-ups. And he is still stronger!

Strength has many dimensions. Love has its own strength. For example, to carry a child in the womb for nine months needs strength, stamina, love. No man could manage it. An artificial womb could be placed in man—now scientific technology has come to the point where man could have a plastic womb implanted, but I don't think he could survive nine months!—they are both going to jump into the ocean.

It is difficult to give life to another soul, to give a body to another soul, to give a brain and mind to another soul. The woman shares wholeheartedly in giving to the child whatever she can manage. And even after the child is born, it is not easy to bring up children. To me, it seems to be the most difficult thing in the world. Astronauts and Edmund Hillary . . . these people should first try to bring up children. Then only can we accept that they have done something by going to Everest; otherwise it is pointless.

Even if you have reached the moon and walked on it, it does not matter. It doesn't show that you are stronger. A living child—so volatile, such an energy overflowing that he will tire you within hours. Nine months in the womb and then a few years . . . .

Just try one night to sleep with a small baby in your bed. During that night, in your house, something is going to happen. Either the child will kill you or you will kill the child. Most probably, you will kill the child, because children are the nastiest people in the world. They are so fresh and they want to do so many things and you are dead tired. You want to go to sleep, and the child is fully awake and he wants to do all kinds of things and he wants your advice, and asks questions . . . and if nothing works then he wants to go to the bathroom! He's feeling thirsty, he's feeling hungry in the middle of the night . . . . The child sleeps the whole day. In the mother's womb, he sleeps twenty-four hours a day; then, slowly slowly . . . twenty-three, twenty-two, twenty, but he is almost always asleep. And in the night, he wakes up. The whole day he will be asleep and in the night he will wake up to torture you.

I don't think there is any man who can have a pregnancy or who can bring up children. It is the strength of the woman. But it is a different strength. There is one strength which is destructive, there is another strength which is creative. There is one strength which is of hatred and there is another strength which is of love.

Love, trust, beauty, sincerity, truthfulness, authenticity— these are all feminine qualities, and they are far greater than any qualities that man has. But the whole past has been dominated by man and his qualities.

Naturally, in war, love is of no use, truth is of no use, beauty is of no use, aesthetic sensibility is of no use. In war, you need a heart which is more stony than stones. You simply require hate, anger, a madness to destroy. In 3,000 years, man has fought 5,000 wars. Yes, this is also strength, but not worthy of human beings. This is strength derived from our animal inheritance. It belongs to the past, which is gone, and the feminine qualities belong to the future, which is coming. What man has to earn, woman has been given by nature as a gift.

Man has to learn how to love. Man has to learn how to let the heart be the master and the mind be just an obedient servant. Man has to learn these things. The woman brings these things with her, but we condemn all these qualities as weaknesses.

Women are women and men are men; there is no question of comparison. Equality is out of the question. They are not unequal and neither can they be equal. They are unique.

Man is not in a better position than woman as far as religious experience is concerned. But he has one quality and that is of the warrior. Once he gets a challenge, then he can develop any kind of qualities. Even the feminine qualities he can grow better than any woman can. His fighting spirit balances things. Women have these qualities inborn. Man needs only to be provoked, given a challenge: these qualities have not been given to you—you have to earn them. And if men and women both can live these qualities, the day is not far away when we can transform this world into paradise.

I would like the whole world to be full of feminine qualities. Then only can wars disappear. Then only can marriage disappear. Then only can nations disappear. Then only can we have one world: a loving, peaceful, silent and beautiful world.

But when I say the man has to grow feminine qualities, I don't mean that he has to imitate women.

12

The Macho

*A woman friend of mine often uses the words
'male ego' about me, which I feel is not true about
me. From the very beginning, I have been open
and vulnerable to feminine energy. Moreover, I
have felt that when she used this word, there was
some kind of hatred towards men. Can you explain
what the 'male ego' is, and what it means when a
woman uses this expression about a man?*

THE EGO IS simply the ego, it is neither male nor female.

But man has been very inhuman towards women for
centuries, continuously. And the strange thing is that man
has been so cruel and inhuman towards women because he
feels a deep inferiority complex in comparison to them.
The greatest problem has been that woman is capable of
becoming a mother; she is capable of giving birth to life,
and man is not. That was the beginning of the feeling of
inferiority—that nature depends on woman, not on man.

Moreover, he has found that she is in many ways
stronger than him. Women are more patient, more tolerant
than men. Men are very impatient and very intolerant.
Women are less violent than men. Women don't commit

murders; it is the man who commits murders, who wages crusades, who is always getting ready for war, who invents all kinds of deadly weapons—atomic bombs, nuclear weapons. The woman is completely out of this whole game of death. Hence, it was no coincidence that man started feeling somehow inferior. And nobody wants to be inferior; the only way was to force the woman in artificial ways to become inferior. For example, not to allow her education, economic freedom, not to let her move out of the house, but confine her to an imprisonment. It seems almost unbelievable what man has done to woman just to get rid of his inferiority. He has made her artificially inferior.

It is not only a question for you. When your woman is telling you that you have a male ego, she is simply representing all women, and you are nothing but a representative of all men. Your forefathers have done so much harm that there is no way to come to a balance. So when your woman says that this is male ego, try to understand—perhaps she is right. Most probably, she is right—because the male has accepted himself as superior for so long that he does not feel that it is his ego. It is the woman who feels it.

Don't deny her feeling. Be grateful to her, and ask where she feels the ego so that you can drop it. Take her help.

You are denying it; you don't feel that you have any male ego. But it is simply a traditional heritage. Every small boy has a male ego. Just a small boy, if he starts crying, you immediately say, 'Why are you crying like a girl? A girl is allowed to cry because she is subhuman. You are going to be a big male chauvinist; you are not supposed to cry or weep.' And small boys start stopping their tears. It is very rare to find men who are as ready to cry and allow tears to flow as women are.

Listen to the woman. You have suppressed and oppressed the woman so much, it is time that she should be listened to and things should be corrected. At least in your personal life do as much as you can to allow the woman as much freedom as possible—the same freedom that you allow yourself. Help her to stand up so that she can blossom again.

We will have a more beautiful world if all women— and women are half of the world—are allowed to grow their talents, their genius. It is not a question at all . . . nobody is higher, nobody is lower. Women are women, men are men; they have differences, but differences don't make anybody higher or lower. Their differences create their attraction. Just think of a world where there are only men. It will be so ugly. Life is rich because there are differences, different attitudes, different opinions. Nobody is superior, nobody is inferior. People are simply different.

Accept this, and help your woman to be free from 10,000 years of repression. Be a friend to her. Much harm has been done; she has been wounded so much that if you can do some healing with your love, you will be contributing to the whole world, to the whole world consciousness.

Don't feel bad if your woman says, 'This is male ego.' It is there in a subtle form, unrecognizable because it has been there for so long; you have forgotten that this is ego. Take her help so that you can recognize it and destroy it.

✳

Why do men have hair on their chests?

Well, they can't have everything!

✳

I always hear you saying nice things about woman.
Could you not stick up for man once in a while?

It is a very difficult question. I could not sleep the whole night. I tried and tried hard to find something nice about man, but I have to admit to you there is nothing that can be said. You can see for yourself:

An interviewer for a ladies' magazine is questioning a famous British general about his sex life. 'Excuse me, sir,' she begins, 'but can you recall the last time you had relations with your wife?'

His upper lip stiffens for a moment and then he says, 'Yes, of course I can, it was nineteen forty-five.'

After a moment's silence, the woman says, 'That was a long time ago.'

The general glances at his watch and says, 'Not so long, really. It is only twenty-one forty-nine.'

Man is a funny thing. If any of you find anything nice about man, please inform me. I accept my failure absolutely.

The world suffers too much from conflict because of male energy and the domination by it. The balance is needed. I am not saying that male energy is not needed at all; it is needed, but in proportion. Right now, 99 per cent is male energy and the woman exists only on the margin. She is not the main current of life, hence there is strife, struggle, fight, war. That energy has brought humanity to the brink of total suicide. It can happen any day, unless the feminine energy is released to balance it. That is the only hope.

World War III can be avoided only if feminine energy is released into the world to balance male energy; otherwise, there is no way. It cannot be avoided by peace marches and protests against war, because that too is male energy! Have you not watched protesters?—they are as violent as anybody can be, and each peace march turns into a riot. Sooner or later, they are burning buses, throwing stones at the police. They are there shouting for peace, but in their very shout is war.

The masculine energy can talk about peace but can only prepare for war. It goes on saying that we have to fight to protect peace. Now look at the absurdity: we have to go to war, otherwise there will be no peace in the world. To attain peace, we go into war. That's how we have been going into war down the ages and peace has not come. Not a single day passes when there is not war somewhere or the other. Sometimes it is Vietnam, sometimes it is Israel, sometimes it is Kashmir, sometimes it is something else, but the war continues. And it is not only a question of changing the political ideology of the world—that won't help because all those ideologies are masculine.

The feminine energy has to be released. That can bring balance. The moon has been neglected too much, the sun has become too prominent. The moon has to be brought back to life. And with the moon is not only the woman: with the moon is poetry too, all aesthetics, all love, and all that belongs to the heart. All that is intuitive feeds on the moon.

Remember this. And in each being, man or woman, both energies exist—the sun and the moon. The emphasis has to be towards the moon. We have leaned too much towards the sun; it is destroying us. Just to keep a balance, we have to lean to the opposite direction, and slowly, slowly one has to be exactly in the middle—the moon in one hand, the sun in the other, but both equal. I declare man and woman equal, not because of any political reason: I declare them equal for some existential reason.

They have to be equal, otherwise life will be destroyed.

So find the woman in you. Feed it, nourish it, help it to grow. Don't be shy of it and don't think, 'I am a man.' Nobody is simply a man and nobody is simply a woman; both are both. It has to be so: half of your being has been contributed by your father and half by your mother. You are the meeting of these two energies. You cannot be just man, you cannot be just woman.

Absorb the woman, enhance and help the woman; become more soft, receptive, passive, loving. Because meditation comes easily when one is passive. It is not an active approach towards life. It is just waiting in openness. Meditation comes—it cannot be brought, it cannot be conquered. One has to surrender to it. That is the meaning of the feminine . . . .

✳

In a therapy group that I did recently, I discovered a lot of violence in myself, and a fear of women. My feeling is that the fear of women is connected with my birth, which I re-experienced in the group and which was very painful to me.

They are all interdependent and connected. The fear of women is basically the fear of the mother. And everybody has to come to a reconciliation with the mother. Unless you are reconciled with the mother, you will never be reconciled with any woman, because every woman again and again reminds you of your mother. Sometimes, it may not be consciously, but unconsciously, it will hit.

And every birth is painful now. Civilization has completely destroyed natural birth. No child is born naturally. The mother is so tense that she does not help the process of birth. In fact, she starts obstructing it. She does not allow the child to go out. She starts closing her womb.

This is in tune with the whole tense life that we are living. The modern idea, the basic idea on which all anxiety is founded, is that we have to fight with life and with nature. So it is nothing special to you. Every child more or less has suffered birth. So the only way is to relive it, to make it completely conscious again. Once you can live it consciously, you can understand and forgive your mother, because that poor woman was suffering. It is not that she has done anything to you, she was herself a victim. Nobody is at fault because the whole situation is faulty. She was loaded with her own birth and she re-enacted it with you. That is the only way she knew how to do it.

So once you become alert, conscious, aware, you can forgive. Not only that, you can feel compassion for her. Once compassion arises in you for your mother, reconciliation has happened. Then you don't carry any grudge, and dropping that grudge suddenly will help you towards other women. You will not be afraid; you will be loving.

A woman is one of the most beautiful phenomenon in the world; not to be compared with anything else. The woman is the masterpiece of God. So if you are afraid of her, you will be scared of God, of love, of prayer. You will be afraid of all that is beautiful, because woman personifies beauty and grace.

And once this happens—that you start flowing towards feminine energy around you—then your violence will disappear. Violence is nothing but energy that has to become love and is not becoming love. Violence is nothing but love unlived. A violent person is one who has too much love-energy and does not know how to release it.

Love is creative, violence is destructive, and creative

energy turns into being destructive if not used. The group has made you aware of some very beautiful, meaningful things.

Many people come to me who say that they are afraid of women, very afraid. Because of that fear, they cannot make a meaningful relationship, they cannot relate; the fear is always there. When you are in fear, the relationship will be contaminated by fear. You will not be able to move totally. You will relate half-heartedly, always afraid: the fear of being rejected, the fear that the woman may say no.

And there are other fears. If a man goes on repeating, 'I am not afraid of women, and every day I am getting better,' if he tries such methods, he can suppress the fear temporarily, but the fear will be there and will come again and again and again.

A man who is afraid of women shows that he must have had some experience with the mother which has caused fear, because the mother is the first woman. In your whole life, you may be related to many women as wife, mistress, daughter, friend, but the image of the mother will persist. That is your first experience. Your whole structure of relationship with women will be based on that foundation, and that foundation is your relationship with your mother. So if a man is afraid of women, he has to be led back, he has to step backwards in memory, he has to go back and find the primal source from where the fear started. It may be an ordinary incident, very minor, he may have completely forgotten it. But if he goes back, he will find the wound somewhere.

You wanted to be loved by the mother, as every child wants, but the mother was not interested. She was a busy woman; she had to attend many associations, clubs, this and that. She was not willing to give the breast to you because she wanted a more proportioned body. She wanted her breasts to be intact and not destroyed by you. She wanted her breasts to be always young so she denied you the breast. Or there may have been other problems in her mind: you were not an accepted child. Like a burden you have come, never wanted in the first place. The pill didn't work and you were born. Or she hated the husband and you had the face of the husband—a deep hatred, or something or the other. But you have to go back and you have to become a child again.

Remember, no stage of life is ever lost. Your child is still within you. It is not that the child becomes the young man, no. The child remains inside, the young man is imposed over it, then the old man is superimposed over the young man, layer by layer. The child never becomes the youth. The child remains there. The young man never becomes the old; another layer, of old age, comes over it. You become like an onion—many layers—and if you penetrate, all the layers are still there, intact.

Primal therapy helps people to go backwards and become children again. They kick, they cry, they weep, they scream, and the scream is no longer of the present. It doesn't belong to the man right now, it belongs to the child who is hidden behind. When that scream, that primal scream comes, many things are immediately transformed.

This is one part of the method of *prati-prasav*. Patanjali, almost 5,000 years ago, taught a system in which every effect had to be led to the cause. Only the cause can be resolved. You can cut the roots, and then the tree will die. But you cannot cut the branches and hope that the tree will die. The tree will thrive more.

Prati-prasav is a beautiful word; *prasav* means birth. When a child is born, it is prasav. Prati-prasav means you are born again in the memory, you go back to the very birth, the trauma when you were born, and you live it again. Remember, you don't remember it, you live it, you relive it again. Remembering is different. You can remember, you can sit silently, but you remain the man you are: you remember that you were a child and were hit hard by your mother. That wound is there, but this is remembering an incident as if it happened to somebody else. To relive it is prati-prasav. To relive it means to become the child again. Not that you remember; you *become* the child again, you live it again. The mother is hitting you not in your memory, the mother hits you again right now: the wound, the anger, the antagonism, your shrinking back, the rejection, and your reaction, as if the whole thing is happening again. This is prati-prasav.

And this is not only as Primal therapy, but as a methodology for every seeker who is in search of the life abundant, of truth.

13

The Beggar

Why am I such a beggar for attention? What can I do about it?

IT IS ONE of the human weaknesses, one of the deep-rooted frailties, to seek attention. The reason one seeks attention is because one does not know oneself. It is only in other people's eyes can one see his face, in their opinions, he can find his personality. What they say matters immensely. If they neglect him, ignore him, he feels lost. If you pass by and nobody takes any attention, you will start losing what you have put together—your personality. It is something that you have put together. You have not discovered it, it is not natural. It is very artificial and very arbitrary.

It is not only you who are a beggar for attention; almost everybody is. And the situation cannot change until you discover your authentic self—which does not depend on anybody's opinion, attention, criticism, indifference, which does not have anything to do with anybody else. Because very few people have been able to discover their reality, the whole world is full of beggars. Deep down, you are all trying to find attention; it is nourishment for your personality. Even if people condemn you, criticize you, are against you, that is acceptable; at least they are paying attention to you. If they are friendly, respectful, of course that is far better, but you cannot survive as a personality without some kind of attention. It can be negative, it can be positive, it doesn't matter. People must say something about you; respectful or disrespectful, they fulfil the same purpose.

I would like you to think about the word *respect*. It does not mean honour, as it is said in all the dictionaries without exception. Respect simply means looking again, re-spect. When you are passing by on the road, somebody looks back again, you have caught his eye—you are somebody. Because respect gives you the idea of being somebody special, you can do anything stupid just to get attention.

In all the ages, people have tried in a thousand and one ways to get attention. Those ways are not necessarily rational—for example, the punks in the West. What do they really want by cutting their hair in strange and weird ways, and then painting it with different psychedelic colours? What do they want? They are beggars. You should not be angry with them because that is what they want. You should not condemn them because that is what they want. Their parents should not criticize them because that is what they want. They cannot survive without people paying attention to them.

In the past, people have done all kinds of things you may not believe. People have remained naked . . . . What was the need for Mahavira or Diogenes to be naked? It is no longer natural for man to be naked in all seasons; he lost that capacity long ago. All animals are naked, but they have a natural immunity. When it is winter, their hair grows, when it is hot in summer, their hair falls. Nature has given them protection. The same protection was available to man too, but man is intelligent and can improve on nature. He found ways to cover his body according to the seasons. Naturally, his body lost the natural growth of hair. Now, to be naked . . . suddenly, your body cannot create the mechanism to protect you.

I know Mahavira or Diogenes are unique individuals, but I think they were a little uncertain of their uniqueness. They fulfilled that suspicion, that missing gap, by being naked, because you cannot avoid giving attention to a naked person in a world where everybody is wearing clothes. The naked person stands aloof. You cannot avoid . . . it is almost irresistible to look at him, to ask, 'What is the matter?' But their nakedness became something spiritual; people started being respectful just because they were naked. Now, nakedness is not a quality or any qualification or any creativity; all animals, birds, trees are naked.

There are still Jaina monks in India, not more than twenty. They used to be in thousands, but now to find that many stupid people is a little difficult. One Jaina monk dies and is not replaced, so their number keeps on falling. Only twenty people all over India are still naked—and I have seen many of them; they don't show any sign of intelligence, they don't show any quality of silence, they don't show any joy. Their faces are sad, dull, sleepy. They are suffering, they are torturing themselves, just for the simple reason that it brings them the attention of people.

Anything, howsoever stupid, is possible for man if it can bring attention to him. In Russia, before the revolution, there was a Christian sect, followers of which used to cut off their genitals publicly on a particular day each year— and they had thousands of followers. Their only qualification for being spiritual was that they had cut off their genitals. When the day arrived, they would gather in a church courtyard and they would cut off their genitals and pile them up. And thousands of people would come to see this stupidity. The women were not left behind . . . of course they were in a difficulty because they don't have hanging genitals to cut off; their genitals are inwards. They started cutting off their breasts—they were not ready to be left behind. It was such a messy and bloody affair, but people were touching their feet, worshipping them, and all that they have done was just an ugly act against nature and against themselves.

What is significant if a man goes on a fast? Mahatma Gandhi used the strategy his whole life: it was nothing but to catch the attention of the whole nation. And if he was going on a fast unto death, the whole world's attention was immediately caught. Otherwise, there is no spirituality in fasting: millions die starving. Millions are going to die from starvation in the coming ten, twelve years. Nobody will give any honour or respect to them. Why? Because their starvation is inevitable. They are not starving wilfully but because they don't have food; they are simply poor and starving people.

But Mahatma Gandhi had everything available to him, although he lived like a poor man. One of his intimate followers, a very intelligent woman, Sarojini Naidu—has a statement on record that to keep Mahatma Gandhi poor, they had to spend treasures on him. It was not simple poverty, it was a managed show.

He would not drink milk from a buffalo because it is rich, rich with Vitamin A and other vitamins. He would not drink the milk of a cow because that too is rich, and poor people cannot afford it. He would drink only the milk of a goat, because that is the cheapest animal and poor people can afford it. But you will be surprised: his goat was being washed twice a day with Lux toilet soap!

His goat's food consisted of the richest nourishment that any rich man may feel jealous of. It is such an insane world! The goat was given the milk of a cow to drink. Cashew nuts, apples and other nourishing fruits were her only food; she was not living on grass. Her daily food in those old days cost Rs 10 per day; in those days that was enough for a man to live for a whole month.

And Gandhi was travelling third class. Naturally, he was attracting attention—a great man is travelling third class! But nobody saw that the third class compartment, which could have carried sixty people at least, was carrying only a single man; it was far more costly than an air-conditioned compartment. But it attracted attention.

He started using clothes just like the farmers of India— they are 80 per cent of the people in the country. Because he was using farmer's clothes—the upper body is naked, only the lower body has a small piece of cloth to wrap around—the poor people of this country became immensely respectful and started calling him *Mahatma*, the great soul. But I have been looking into his life as deeply as possible. I don't find any great soul; I have not found even a little soul—just pure politics in the name of religion. Knowing perfectly well that India can be impressed only by religion, he was singing devotional songs every day in the morning and in the evening, but it was all to attract attention.

Attention gives you tremendous nourishment for the ego.

Politicians can pretend to be religious if religion is attractive. Because they need attention, their whole personality is false. It depends on how many people are following them; it depends on the number of people who are attentive to them. It is a politics of numbers.

The Catholic pope is against birth control, against abortion, not because he is compassionate, saying, 'This is absolute cruelty and violence,' not because he is life-affirmative—the whole Catholic attitude is life-negative, it is against life. Then why is there this insistence that there should be no birth control and no abortion? Because this is the only way to increase the number of Catholics, and to make other people so poor that they have to come under the fold of the Catholic empire.

Now that there are so many orphans in India, Catholics have a good opportunity. And one wonders . . . a woman like Mother Teresa is awarded a Nobel prize, is given many doctorates in India by Indian universities, is awarded prizes by the Indian government, all because she is taking care of orphans. But nobody thinks that this care simply means converting those orphans to Catholics. Naturally, Mother Teresa cannot be in favour of birth control—from where will she get the orphans?

Christianity cannot be in favour of a world which is rich. The scientists declare continually that we have come to such a point of technological progress that now there is no need for anybody to be hungry, to starve or die because of shortage of food. It has never before been possible, but now scientists are saying that we can feed five billion people very easily, we can feed even more—but those voices are silenced. No politician pays any attention, because politicians are interested in having a big following.

Your so-called religious leaders, your so-called political leaders, all need attention, all need their names and their photos continually in newspapers, because if newspapers forget anybody's name for a few months, people forget that man also. Now what do you know about Richard Nixon? Where is that poor fellow? One day he was the greatest, most powerful man on the earth, and now you will only hear about him the day he dies, and that too will be on the third, fourth page of newspapers in a small column. What happens to these powerful people? When they lose people's attention, their personality starts disappearing.

I have known many political leaders in this country. Perhaps this country has more ex-ministers, chief ministers, governors than any other country. Once they become 'ex' they are finished. Then nobody pays any attention to them, nobody asks them to inaugurate bridges, railway lines, hospitals, schools. No paper even bothers where they are, whether they are alive or dead. And there was a time when they were in newspapers every day, on radios, on television.

It is not only your problem, that you are a beggar for attention; it is a human reality. And the reason is that you depend on your personality—which is false, which has been created by society, and which can be taken away by society. Don't depend on it. It is not in your power. That which is in your power is your own individuality. Discover it! And the name of the science to discover it is meditation.

Once you know yourself, you don't care about others. Even if the whole world forgets you, it does not matter, it does not even make the slightest difference to you; or the whole world can know—that too does not give you any ego. You know ego is false, and to depend on the false is to make houses on sand, without foundation. Your personalities are almost signatures on water. You have not even signed, and they disappear.

A group of Jewish mothers was drinking coffee together, and bragging about their children. One had a four-year-old who could read already. Another had a five-year-old who had appeared on television.

Then Becky Goldberg spoke up and said, 'That's nothing. You should see my little Hymie. He is only five years old, but the other day he went to the psychiatrist all by himself!'

A middle-aged woman confessed to her priest that she was becoming vain.

'Why do you think so?' asked the priest.

'Because,' replied the woman, 'every time I look in the mirror, I am inspired by my beauty.'

'Don't worry,' said the priest, 'that's not a sin, that's only a mistake!'

It was a big meeting of the medical society in honour of an ear specialist who was retiring after more than fifty years of service. As a gift, they presented him with a golden ear.

He stood up to make a speech, and after the applause died down, looked at his gift and said, 'Thank God I was not a gynaecologist!'

Don't depend on others! Be independent in your being. Just listen to your inner voice.

You can listen the moment you start stilling and silencing your mind—and it is not difficult. And when I say it is not difficult, I say it with absolute authority: it is not difficult! If it has happened to me, it can happen to you—there is no difference. All human beings are potentially capable of knowing themselves. And the moment you know yourself, then nobody can take away your individuality. Even if they kill you, they can only kill the body, not you.

An individual is the only person who can get rid of this state of begging; otherwise, you are going to remain a beggar your whole life. But if you want to get rid of this begging, you will have to get rid of your ego and your personality. You will have to learn that there is nothing in respect, reputation or respectability. They are all bogus words, meaningless, contentless. The reality belongs to you, but unless you discover it, you will have to depend on others.

You are emperors, but you have to discover yourself. And this discovery is not difficult: your kingdom is within you. You just have to learn to close your eyes and look inwards. A little discipline, a little learning not to remain focused on the outside continuously, but to turn inwards at least once or twice a day, whenever you can find time . . . Slowly, slowly you start becoming aware of your eternal being. Then the idea of attention simply disappears. And the miracle is: the day you don't need anybody's attention, people start feeling your charisma, because charisma is the radiation of your individuality. They start feeling that you are somebody special, unique—although they cannot pinpoint where your uniqueness is, what it is that attracts like a magnet.

People who have discovered themselves have found thousands of people attracted towards them, but they are not asking for it.

14

The Boyfriend

My girlfriend told me I am a little boring, not very juicy, very dependent and a victim. I observed in myself this destructive energy and I felt that I somehow enjoyed it! Is it possible to use this energy in some creative way?

YOUR GIRLFRIEND IS very compassionate, because each man finally becomes very boring, not a little boring. Do you realize that what you call love is a repetition, the same stupid gymnastics again and again? And in this whole game, the man is the loser. He is dissipating his energy, perspiring, huffing, puffing, and the girl keeps her eyes closed, thinking, 'It is a question only of two or three minutes and this nightmare will be finished.'

People are so non-inventive that they take it for granted that going through the same actions is making them more interesting. That's why I say your girlfriend is very compassionate—she only told you that you are a little boring. I say to you, you are *utterly* boring.

When the Christian missionaries came to this country, people discovered that they knew only one posture of making love—the woman underneath and those ugly beasts on top of the delicate woman. In India, that posture is called the missionary posture. India is an ancient land and the birthplace of many sciences, particularly sexology. A book of tremendous importance, by Vatsyayana, has been in existence for 5,000 years. The name of the book is *Kama Sutra*, hints for making love. And it comes from a man of deep meditation—he has created eighty-four postures for lovemaking. Naturally, the love posture should change; otherwise you are bound to be boring.

Vatsyayana recognizes the fact that the same love posture creates boredom, a feeling of utter stupidity, because you are always doing the same thing. He invented eighty-four postures to make the love life of couples a little interesting. Nobody in the whole world has written a book of the calibre of *Kama Sutra*. But it could only have come from a man of immense clarity, of deep meditativeness.

What is your lovemaking? If you look at your lovemaking, you yourself will feel that it is all boring. And particularly for the woman it is more boring, because the man is finished in two or three minutes and the woman has not even started. And all around the world, cultures have enforced in the minds of women that they are not supposed even to enjoy or move or be playful—that is called 'dirty'; prostitutes do it, not ladies. Ladies have to lie down almost dead and let that old guy do whatsoever he wants to do; it is nothing new, there is nothing new even to see.

You should not take it as a personal disrespect. Your girlfriend is telling you something really sincere and honest. Have you given her orgasmic joy? Or have you only used her to throw out your sexual energy? Have you reduced her to a commodity? She has been conditioned to accept it, but even this accepting cannot be joyful.

You make love on the same bed where you fight every day. In fact, fighting is the preface: throwing pillows, shouting at each other, arguing about everything and then, feeling tired, some negotiation is needed. Your love is only a negotiation. If you are a man of aesthetic sensibility, your love chamber should be a sacred place, because it is in that love chamber that life is born. It should have beautiful flowers, incense, fragrance; you should enter into it with deep respect.

And love should not be just an abrupt thing—grab the woman. This hit-and-run affair is not love. Love should have a preface of beautiful music, of dancing together, of meditating together. And love should not be a mind thing—that you are continuously thinking of how to make love and then go to sleep. Love should be a deeper involvement of your whole being, and it should not be projected by the mind, but should come out spontaneously. Beautiful music, fragrance, you are dancing hand in hand, you have again become small children playing with flowers . . . . If spontaneously love happens in this sacred atmosphere, it will have a different quality.

You should understand that woman is capable of multiple orgasms because she does not lose any energy. Man is capable of only one orgasm and he loses energy, looks depressed. Even the next morning you can see his hangover, and as he goes on growing older, it becomes more and more difficult. This difference has to be understood. The woman is on the receptive end—she has to be because she has to become a mother, she needs more energy. But her orgasm has a totally different way of happening. Man's sexuality is local, like local anaesthesia. A woman's body is sexual all over, and unless her whole body starts trembling with joy, each cell of her body starts becoming involved, she cannot have an orgasmic explosion.

So it is not only in your case, it is the case for almost 99 per cent of women around the world. The whole situation has to be changed. The woman should not be under the man. In the first place it is ugly—man has a stronger body, the woman is more fragile. She should be on top of the man, not the man on top of the woman.

Secondly, man should remain silent, inactive, so that his orgasm is not finished within two minutes. If you are silent and let the woman go crazy on top of your chest, it will give her good exercise and will bring her to an explosion of orgasmic energy. It takes time for her whole body to warm up, and if you are not inactive, there is no time. So you meet, but the meeting is not of beauty, of love, but just utilitarian.

Try with your girlfriend what I am saying. You be the inactive partner and let her be the active partner. Allow her to be uninhibited. She has not to behave like a lady, she has to behave like an authentic woman. The lady is just created by man; woman is created by existence. You have to fill the gap between her orgasms. The gap can be filled in only one way, that you remain very inactive, silent, and enjoy her going crazy. And she will have multiple orgasms. You should end the game with your orgasm, but you should not begin with it.

And your woman will not call you a little boring. You will be a really interesting, real wonderful guy who is behaving like a lady! Keep your eyes closed so that she is not inhibited by your eyes. So she can do anything— movement of the hands, movement of the body, moaning, groaning, shouting. Until she says, '*Hari Om Tat Sat!*' you are not allowed to be alive, you simply remain silent. This should be the indication. '*Hari Om Tat Sat*' simply means: this orgasmic explosion, this is the truth. Then she will be mad after you. Right now, you must be behaving stupidly, as most of the men in the world do.

The second thing you say, '*My girlfriend is saying that I am not very juicy.*' So become a little more juicy! To become juicy is not very difficult. The juice of all kinds of fruits is available everywhere. Drink more juice, less solid food. She is giving you good advice and you in your stupidity are thinking that she is condemning you.

When she says, '*You are very dependent and a victim,*' I can see even through your question that she is right. A victim you are, just as every human being is a victim—a victim of stupid ideologies, which have created strange guilt feelings and do not allow you to be playful. Although you may be making love, you know you are committing a sin and that hell is not far off.

Becky Goldberg was telling Goldberg, 'You are a great lover!'

Goldberg said, 'But you never told me this before. I was waiting for somebody to say that I am a great lover, but I dropped the idea because it seems I am not.'

Becky Goldberg said to him, 'No, you are a great lover, and I wanted to say it to you many times, but you were not there!'

Making love to Becky . . . and Goldberg is not there. He is counting his money, doing his accounts, and his mind is doing thousands of things.

In every bed where there are two lovers, there are at least—I mean, minimum—four people. There are more inventive people, they may have a whole crowd in the bed. The woman is making love to Goldberg and thinking of Muhammad Ali. Goldberg is making love as a duty and is thinking of so many beautiful actresses; but his mind is not there, and neither is his wife's mind there. Their minds are in their dreams.

A man told his friend, 'Last night, I had a tremendous dream. I have to tell you. I have been waiting for the morning to tell you the dream.'

The man asked, 'What kind of dream?'

He said, 'I went fishing in my dream and I caught such big fish that even to draw in one big fish was a strenuous job for me. And I caught so many fish! I don't know where these fish disappear in the day.'

The other man said, 'Stop all this nonsense, you don't know what I have dreamt. I found in my dream, on one side of me, Sophia Loren, absolutely nude. And I said, "My God, have I reached heaven?" And on the other side was another beautiful woman. It was impossible to judge who was more beautiful.'

The friend became very angry and said, 'You idiot! You pretend to be my best friend. Why didn't you call me?'

He said, 'I did call, but your wife said you had gone fishing.'

Nobody is where you think he is. Nobody is at home. While making love, make it a meditative process. Your whole presence has to be there, showering on the woman you love. The woman has to be there, showering all her beauty and grace on her lover. Then you will not be a victim, otherwise you are a victim.

Love is not accepted by your so-called, utterly idiotic religions to be a natural and playful experience. They condemn it. They have made it a condition: unless you leave your woman, you will never attain truth. And the conditioning has been going on for so long that it has almost become a truth, although it is an absolute lie. You are a victim of traditions and you are certainly dependent.

You are saying, '*I observed in me this destructive energy and I felt that I somehow enjoyed it.*' Everybody has destructive energy, because energy, if left to itself, is bound to be destructive—unless it is used with awareness and becomes creative.

But the most important thing that you are saying is, '*Somehow I enjoyed it.*' Then how are you going to change it? With anything that you enjoy, you are bound to remain on the same level; you cannot change it, because you may not enjoy the change. You have energy. To enjoy destructive energy is suicidal, to do so is being in the service of death. If you are aware of it, you have to go through a transformation. Use your energy creatively. Perhaps that will make you less boring, more juicy, less dependent, less of a victim.

And the most important part is that you will not feel guilty and depressed. No creative person feels depressed and guilty. His participation in the universe by his creative actions makes him tremendously fulfilled and gives him dignity. That is the very birthright of every man, but very few people claim it.

And there is no difficulty, it is so easy to use energy in creative fields. Paint, do gardening, grow flowers, write poetry, learn music, dance. Learn anything that changes your destructive energy into creative energy. Then you will not be angry at existence or against life, you will be grateful. How can a creative person be against life, love? It is impossible, it has never happened. It is only the uncreative people who are against everything.

Your girl has raised very important questions for your life. The easiest way would be to change the girlfriend, but I suggest that your girlfriend is certainly a friend to you and that whatever she has said is absolutely sincere, authentic. Be grateful to her and start changing things. The day your girlfriend accepts you as juicy, as interesting, will be a great day in your life. So don't be a coward and change girlfriends just because this girlfriend creates trouble in your mind, and you want to find some other girlfriend.

You are fortunate to find a very compassionate girl. Your next choice will be very difficult; she will make you feel absolutely guilty and unworthy. Because what have you done to be worthy? What have you done not to be boring? What have you done to declare your independence? What have you done not to be a victim? It is time you should do it. You will remain always grateful to your girlfriend.

I would like to tell your girlfriend, 'Go on hitting this fellow until you are satisfied that he is not boring, but full of juice, utterly interesting, playful, celebrating. You may lose him somewhere on the path of life, but you will have prepared him for some other woman; otherwise the way he is now, he is going to torture many women and torture himself.'

15

The Husband

*I am a married man with three children and with
all the problems of a married man's life. My wife
is constantly at my throat. We are together only
for the sake of the children; otherwise, each moment
is a nightmare. Is there any chance of my escaping
hellfire?*

I WILL TELL you one story:

A man was arraigned before an Arkansas justice on the
charge of obtaining money under false pretenses. The
judge looked at him thoughtfully. 'Your name is Jim
Moore?'

'Yes, sir.'

'You are charged with a crime that merits a long term
in the penitentiary?'

'Yes, sir.'

'You are guilty of that crime?'

The man squared his shoulders doggedly. 'I am.'

'You ask me for mercy?'

'No, sir.'

The judge smiled grimly. 'You have had a great deal of

trouble within the last two years?'

'I have.'

'You have often wished you were dead?'

'I have, please Your Honour.'

'You wanted to steal enough money to take you far away from Arkansas?'

'You are right, Judge.'

'If a man had stepped up and shot you as you entered the store, you would have said, "Thank you, sir"?'

'Why, yes, I would. But, Judge, how in the world did you find out so much about me?'

'Some time ago,' said the Judge, with a solemn air, 'I divorced my wife. Shortly afterwards, you married her. The result is conclusive. I discharge you. Here, take this $50 bill. You have suffered enough.'

You need not be worried about hell: you have suffered enough, you are already in it. You can only go to heaven, because nothing else is left. Celibates may go to hell, but you cannot. You have suffered enough. Celibates may need a little taste of suffering, but not you.

In fact, there is no hell somewhere else and no heaven either. Hell is here, heaven is here. Hell and heaven are your ways of being. They are your ways of living. You can live in such a way that the whole life is a benediction. But don't go on throwing the responsibility only on your wife. In the first place, it is you who have chosen her. Why have you chosen such a wife who is constantly at your neck?

And do you think, if you are divorced, you will not again choose another woman of the same type? If you ask psychologists, they will say you will again choose the same type of woman. You needed it; it is your own choice. You cannot live without misery. You think your wife is creating misery? It is because you wanted to live in misery—that's why you have chosen this woman. You will again choose the same type of woman. You will only become attracted to the same type of woman unless you drop your old mind completely.

Except our own minds, there is no other way to change or transform. You must be thinking that if you divorce this woman, things will be good. You are wrong, you are utterly wrong. You don't know a thing about human psychology. You will get trapped again. You will search for a woman again; you will miss this woman very much. She will miss you, you will miss her. You will again find the same type of person; you will be attracted only to that kind of person. Watch your mind.

And then, only she cannot be at fault; you must be doing something to her too. It is your statement; I don't know her statement. It will be unfair to the poor woman if I accept your statement about her totally. You may be 50 per cent right, but what about the other 50 per cent? You must be supplying fuel to the fire. And if life was so ugly, why have you given birth to three children? Who is responsible for that? Why have you brought three souls into the ugly world of your family, into the nightmare that you are living? Why? Can't you have any love for your children?

People go on reproducing without thinking of what they are doing. If your life is such a hell, at least you could have prevented your children from falling into the trap of your misery. You would have saved them! Now, those three children are being brought up by two persons like you and your wife. They will learn ways and means from you, and they will perpetuate you in the world. When you are gone, you will still be here in the world creating hell. Those children will perpetuate, they will keep the continuity of your stupid ways of living, miserable ways of living.

Now your boy will find a woman just like your wife— who else?—because he will know only this woman. He will love his mother, and whenever he falls in love with a woman, it simply means that woman reminds him of his mother. Now again the same game will be played. Maybe you have chosen your wife according to your mother; your father and your mother were playing the same game that you are playing, and your children will perpetuate the same structure and the same gestalt. That's how miseries persist.

At least you could have saved these three children's lives, and you could have saved the future of humanity, because the ripple that you have created will go on and on. Even when you are gone, it will be there. Whatsoever you do abides. Whatsoever ripples you create in the ocean of life remain; you disappear. It is like throwing a stone in a silent lake: the stone falls deep into the lake, disappears, goes to the bottom and rests there, but the ripples that have been created, they go on spreading towards the shores. And the ocean of life knows no shores, so those waves go on and on, forever and forever. At least you could have been a little more alert not to produce children. And it is never late. Still life can be changed—but don't hope that your wife should change. That is the wrong approach.

You change. Change radically. Stop doing things that you have always been doing. Start doing things that you have never done. Change radically, become a new person, and you will be surprised. When you become a new person, your wife becomes a new person. She will have to, to respond to you. In the beginning, she will find it hard because it will almost be like living with another husband, but slowly, slowly she will see that if you can change, why can't she? Never hope that the other should change. In every relationship, start the change from your side.

Life can still become a paradise; it is never too late. But great courage is needed to change. All that is really needed is a little more awareness. De-automatize your behaviour; just watch what you have been doing up to now. You do the same thing, and the wife reacts in the same way. It has become a settled pattern.

Watch any husband and wife—they are almost predictable. In the morning, the husband will spread his newspaper and start reading, and the wife will say the same thing that she has been saying for years, and her husband will react in the same way. It has become almost structured, programmed.

Just small changes, and you will be surprised. Tomorrow, don't sit in your chair early in the morning, reading your paper. Just start cleaning the house, and see what happens. Your wife will be wide-eyed, and she will not be able to believe what has happened to you. Smile when you see your wife, hug, and see how she is taken aback. You have never hugged her. Years have passed, and you have never looked into the poor woman's eyes.

Tonight, just sit in front of her, look into her eyes. She will think in the beginning that you have gone crazy, you have become an Osho freak or something, but don't be worried. Just hold her hand and be ecstatic. If you cannot be, at least pretend. Be ecstatic. Sometimes it happens that if you start pretending, it starts happening! Just start smiling, for no reason at all, and watch. Your poor woman may have a heart attack!

You have not been holding her hand—do you remember since how long? Have you ever taken her for a morning walk? Or when the moon is full, have you taken her for a walk in the night under the stars? She is also human, she also needs love. But particularly people in India go on using women as if they are just servants. Their whole work consists of taking care of the children and the kitchen and the house, as if that's their whole life. Have you respected your wife as a human being? Then, if anger arises, it is natural. If she feels frustrated—because her life is running out and she has not known any joy, she has not known any bliss, she has not known anything that can give meaning and significance to her life . . . .

Have you just sat by her side sometimes, silently, just holding her hand, not saying a word, just feeling her, and letting her feel you? Wives and husbands have only one kind of communication: quarrelling. Don't think that only your wife is responsible. She may be, but that is not the point, because she has not asked the question. You have asked the question. Start changing your life. Give the poor woman a little feeling of significance. Give the little woman a little feeling that she is needed. Do you know the greatest need in life is to be needed? And unless a person feels that he or she is needed, his or her life remains meaningless, desert-like.

Laugh with her, listen to music together, go for a holiday. Caress her body, because bodies start shrinking when nobody caresses them. Bodies start becoming ugly if nobody looks at them with appreciation. And then you think, 'Why is my wife not beautiful?' You are not creating the climate in which beauty flowers, blooms. If you love a person, the person immediately becomes beautiful! Love is such an alchemical process. Look at a person with loving eyes, and suddenly you will see his or her aura changing, the face becoming radiant, more blood coming to the face, eyes becoming more shiny, radiance, intelligence—and like a miracle.

Love is a miracle, love is magical. It is not yet too late.

✳

What are the essential things to keep one's wife happy?

I don't know much about wives. I am an unmarried man. You are asking the question to a wrong person. But I have been observing many wives and many husbands. So this is not my experience—just my opinion!

There are two things necessary to keep one's wife happy. First: let her think she is having her own way. And second: let her have it.

Eunice came home with a brand-new mink coat. 'Where did you get that?' asked her husband, Bernie.

'I won it in a raffle,' she replied. The following night, Eunice walked in with a beautiful diamond bracelet.

'Where did that come from?' asked Bernie. 'I won it in a raffle,' said Eunice. 'I'm going to another raffle party tonight, and I'm in a hurry. Would you mind drawing my bath?'

Bernie did as instructed, but when Eunice came in to take her bath, she found that there was only half an inch of water in the tub.

'Bernie,' she asked, 'Why didn't you fill the tub?' 'Well, darling,' he answered, 'I didn't want you to get your raffle ticket wet!'

16

The Father

THE INSTITUTION OF father is something invented by man. It is not a natural thing at all, it is institutional. Some day it may disappear . . . because there was a time when it was not there. For thousands of years, humanity lived without the institution of fatherhood.

You may be surprised to know that the word *uncle* is older than the word *father*, because matriarchy preceded patriarchy. The mother was there and the father was not known, because the mother was meeting, merging, melting with many people. Somebody had to be the father, but there was no way to find out. So all were uncles—all potential fathers were uncles. The institution of fatherhood came into existence with the invention of private property; they are joined together. The father represents private property, because when private property came into existence, everybody wanted his own child to inherit it. 'I will not be here, but a part of me should inherit my property.' Private property came first, then came the father.

And to be absolutely certain that 'The child is my own,' the idea became prevalent in almost all societies of the world that before marriage, the woman has to be absolutely a virgin; otherwise it is difficult to decide. She might already be carrying a child when she gets married, she may already be pregnant, and then the child will be somebody else's and *he* will inherit the property. To make sure that 'It is my child that is going to inherit my property,' virginity was imposed on women.

It is the whole idea of private property that has created the father, that has created the family, that has created the ownership of the woman by the man. If there was a time when there was no father, no private property, a day is bound to come when there will be no private property— the father will disappear.

Hindus have been saying that unless a woman becomes a mother, she is not fulfilled. The same is not true for men—no one will say that unless a man becomes a father, he is not fulfilled. To be a father is accidental. It may be, it may not be. It is not very basic, and a man can remain without being a father without losing anything. But a woman will lose something because her whole creativity, her whole functioning, comes only when she becomes a mother. When her breasts become the centre of her being, she becomes total. And she cannot come to the breasts unless a child is there to call her to them. So men marry women to get wives, and women marry men to become mothers—not to get husbands. Their basic, sole interest is to have a child who will call up their womanhood. So husbands are always afraid, because the moment a child is born, they move to the periphery of the woman's interest— the child becomes the centre.

So fathers always feel jealous because the children come in-between and now the woman is more interested in the children than in the father of the children. He has become a peripheral existence—necessary for survival but non-essential.

Christianity, I have been told by Christian friends, is

based on the family: the family is its foundation stone. But the family is also the foundation stone of all neurosis, of all psychosis, of all kinds of mental sicknesses, of all kinds of social problems. It is also the base of races, nations and wars.

The family has to be understood. It has no future; it has already outlived its usefulness, its necessity. But we have been conditioned—not only Christians, but everybody—that the family is a great contribution to the world. The reality is totally different. I have to go point by point, in detail, because the problem of family is one of the most serious problems.

The first thing . . . . The family is a prison, it wants to keep control of the children, of the wife. It is a very tight group of people, and they have made this prison sacred. But the results are very ugly.

Every kind of imprisonment prevents spiritual growth. What do you think: why did Buddha renounce the world? Why did Mahavira renounce the world? In fact, they were not renouncing the world, they were simply renouncing the family—nobody has said this before—because how can you renounce the world? Wherever you are, the world is. You can only renounce the family. But all religious scriptures, including Christian scriptures, are continuously lying to the people: they talk of renouncing the world. It distracts you completely from the fact that all these people were renouncing the *family*, because the family was such that they could not grow within it.

The family is programming every child according to its prejudices. If you are born in a Christian family, you will be continuously programmed for Christianity, and you will not suspect that your conditioning may be wrong, your conditioning may be preventing you from going beyond.

Christianity and all other religions go on confusing

people's minds. They never make the distinction between believing and knowing. A blind man can believe in light, but that is not going to help. One needs eyes to see the light, and then there is no need to believe. When you *know* something, is there any need to believe in it?

Do you 'believe' in light? Do you believe in the moon? Do you believe in the stars? You simply know, there is no question of belief. Belief arises only for fictions, for lies, not for truth. Every belief system is a hindrance for spirituality.

Death, according to Christianity, is a taboo: you should not talk about it. Death is taboo, and life is also taboo: you should not live it! Death you should not talk about, and life you should not live! They don't leave you with any alternative—you can neither live, nor can you die. They keep you hanging in the middle, half-dead, half-alive.

This creates schizophrenia. You are not allowed to be total in anything: in life, in death, in love—only partially involved. A man who is partially involved is not fully alive. The deeper your involvement in existence, the deeper your life. When you are involved totally in life, in death, in love, in meditation, in any kind of thing that you want to do— painting, music, poetry, dance . . . . Unless you are totally involved in it, you will never know the maximum, the optimum pleasure, the optimum blissfulness.

People are living only at the minimum, just surviving, or to be absolutely truthful, just vegetating—just waiting and waiting, and nothing happens in their life. No flowers blossom in their life, no festivals happen in their life. And their death is as ugly as their life was, because death is the ultimate culmination of your life.

If you have lived totally, death is not the end. Death is only an episode, a small episode in an eternal life. You have died many times, but because you have never lived totally, you became unconscious at the moment of death; the fear brought you into a coma. That's why you don't remember your past lives—because the coma stands as a barrier for past lives and their remembrance. And because you don't know your past lives, you cannot understand that there is going to be life after death, that life is eternal. Birth and death are mere episodes; thousands of times you have been into birth, into death. But when you are not allowed to live totally, when everywhere there is interference from religion . . . .

On his first day at school, a small boy—a Christian boy—was asked by the teacher, 'What is your name?'

He said, 'Don't.'

The teacher said, 'Strange, I have never heard such a name.'

He said, 'Everything, whatever I do, I only hear this, "Don't"—so I think it is my name.'

But the whole of Christianity is doing that to everybody. It is a life-negative religion, it does not allow you to live joyously. And the family is the root, because obviously the programming starts from the family. Christianity says that it is founded on the family.

And I know perfectly well that unless the family disappears from the world, these religions, these nations, these wars will not disappear, because they are all based on family. The family teaches you that you are a Hindu, and the Hindu religion is the best religion of all; other religions are so-so.

Christianity continues the programming of children, 'You can be saved only through Jesus Christ. Nobody else can save you. All other religions are just moralities, very superficial, they are not going to help you.' And when a child, alongside his breast feeding, is continuously fed with all kinds of superstitions—God, and the Holy Ghost, and the only begotten son of God, Jesus, heaven and hell . . .

Children are very vulnerable because they are born as a *tabula rasa*—nothing is written on them, their minds are pure. You can write anything you want on the child. And every family commits the crime: they destroy the individual and create a slave. Obedience is virtue, disobedience is the original sin.

When a child starts being programmed from his very birth, when he is very vulnerable and very soft, you could write anything. It will go on in his unconscious. You can tell him that 'Our nation is the greatest nation in the world'; every nation is saying that. 'Our religion is the greatest religion, our scripture is written by God himself'— Hindus are saying that, Christians are saying that, Jews are saying that. Everybody is committing the same crime.

Christianity, of course, is doing it more efficiently, more cunningly, because it is the greatest religion in the world. It uses ultra-modern techniques of programming. It sends its missionaries to learn psychoanalysis, to learn how to programme people, how to deprogramme people. If a Hindu has to be converted to Christianity, first he has to be deprogrammed of Hinduism. Again the *tabula rasa* appears; what was written is erased. Now you can write, 'Christianity is the highest religion in the world, and there has been no man like Jesus Christ, and will never be again, because he is the only begotten son of God.'

All wars depend on the family. It has been a tradition in many nations in the past that you contribute at least one son to the army, to protect the nation, to protect the dignity and the pride of the nation. In Tibet, every family contributes the eldest son to the monasteries. This has been done for thousands of years. As if the children are just commodities you can contribute, as if the children mean money which you can give in charity!

This divided the world into different camps because of religion, because of politics, because of nationalities, because of races. They all depend on family. The family is the root cause of mankind's thousands of wounds.

The family gives you ambition, it gives you desires, it gives you a longing to be successful, and all these things create tensions, anxieties: how can one be a celebrity? The family wants you to be a celebrity. The family wants you to be known all over the world. The family wants you to be the richest person. The family wants you to be the president of the country. All these ambitions the family creates, without knowing that all these ambitions are creating a mind which will remain continuously in anguish, suffering. Only one man can become the president of the country. What about the other nine hundred million people in India?—they are all failures. This is an ugly situation, to keep people feeling they are failures, unsuccessful, inferior to others.

The family is the base for all pathology.

I would love a world where the family is replaced by the commune. Psychologically, it is more healthy to have a commune, where children are not possessed by the parents, they belong to the commune; where children are not given the imprint of the mother and father only, they have many uncles in the commune, many aunts in the commune. Sometimes they sleep with this family, sometimes with that family. I want the family to be replaced by the commune, and in a commune, there is no need for marriage.

17

The Friend

My love-life drama now reflects an old saying of Humphrey Bogart's, 'Women—they're hell to live with, and hell to live without.' What to do?

ONE HAS TO pass through this hell. One has to experience both the hell of living with a woman and the hell of living without a woman. And it is not only true about women, it is absolutely true about men too. So don't be a male chauvinist pig! It is applicable both ways, it is a double-edged sword. Women are also tired of living with men and they too are frustrated when they have to live alone. It is one of the most fundamental of human dilemmas; it has to be understood. You cannot live without a woman because you don't know how to live with yourself. You are not meditative enough.

Meditation is the art of living with yourself. It is nothing else than that, simply that: the art of being joyously alone. A meditator can sit joyously alone for months, for years. He does not hanker for the other because his own inner ecstasy is so much, is so overpowering, who bothers about the other? If the other comes into his life, it is not a need, it is a luxury. And I am all for luxury, because luxury means you can enjoy it if it is there and you can enjoy it when it is not there. But a need is a difficult phenomenon. For example, bread and butter are needs, but the flowers in the garden are a luxury. You can live without the flowers, you will not die, but you cannot live without bread and butter.

For the man who cannot live with himself, the other is a need, an absolute need, because whenever he is alone, he is bored with himself—so bored that he wants some occupation with somebody else. Because it is a need, it becomes a dependence, you have to depend on the other. And because it becomes a dependence, you hate, you rebel, you resist, because it is a slavery. Dependence is a kind of slavery, and nobody wants to be a slave.

You meet a woman—you are not able to live alone. The woman is also not able to live alone, that's why she is meeting you; otherwise there is no need. Both are bored with themselves and both are thinking that the other will help to get rid of the boredom. Yes, in the beginning, it looks like that, but only in the beginning. As they settle together, soon they see that the boredom is not destroyed— it is not only doubled but multiplied. Now, first they were bored with themselves, now they are bored with the other too—because the closer you come to the other, the more you know the other, the more the other becomes almost a part of you. That's why if you see a bored couple walking by, you can be certain they are married. If they are not bored, you can be certain they are not married. The man must be walking with somebody else's wife, that's why there is so much joy.

When you are in love—when you have not yet persuaded the woman and the woman has not yet persuaded you to be together forever—you both pretend great joy. And something of it is true, too, because of the hope that

'Who knows, I may come out of my boredom, my anguish, my anxiety, my aloneness. This woman may help me.' And the woman is also hoping. But once you are together, the hopes soon disappear, despair sets in again. Now you are bored and the problem has become multiplied. Now, how to get rid of this woman?

Because you are not meditative, you need others to keep you occupied. And because you are not meditative, you are not able to love either, because love is an overflowing joy. You are bored with yourself; what have you got to share with the other? Hence, being with the other also becomes hell.

In that sense, Jean-Paul Sartre is right that 'The other is hell.' The other is not hell really, it only appears so. The hell exists in you, in your non-meditativeness, in your incapacity to be alone and ecstatic. And both are unable to be alone and ecstatic. Now both are at each other's throats, continuously trying to snatch some happiness from each other. Both are doing that and both are beggars.

I have heard:

One psychoanalyst met another psychoanalyst on the street. The first one said to the other, 'You look fine. How am I?'

Nobody knows about himself, nobody is acquainted with himself. We only see the faces of others. A woman looks beautiful, a man looks beautiful, smiling, all smiles. We don't know his anguish. Maybe all those smiles are just a facade to deceive others and to deceive himself. Maybe behind those smiles there are great tears. Maybe he is afraid if he does not smile, he may start weeping and crying. When you see the other, you simply see the surface, you fall in love with the surface. But when you come closer, you soon know that the inner depths of the other person are as dark as your own. He is a beggar just as you are. Now . . . two beggars begging from each other. Then it becomes hell.

Yes, you are right, '*Women—they're hell to live with, and hell to live without.*'

It is not a question of women at all, nor a question of men; it is a question of meditation and love. Meditation is the source from which joy wells up within you and starts overflowing. If you have joy enough to share, your love will be a contentment. If you don't have joy enough to share, your love is going to be tiring, exhausting, boring. So whenever you are with a woman, you are bored and want to get rid of her, and whenever you are alone, you are bored with yourself and want to get rid of your loneliness, and you seek and search for a woman. This is a vicious circle! You can go on moving like a pendulum from one extreme to the other your whole life.

See the real problem. The real problem has nothing to do with man and woman. It has something to do with meditation and the flowering of meditation in love, in joy, in blissfulness.

First meditate, be blissful, then much love will happen of its own accord. Then being with others is beautiful and being alone is also beautiful. Then it is simple, too. You don't depend on others and you don't make others dependent on you. Then it is always friendship, friendliness. It never becomes a relationship, it is always a relatedness. You relate, but you don't create a marriage. Marriage is out of fear, relatedness is out of love.

You relate; as long as things are moving beautifully, you share. And if you see that the moment has come to depart, because your paths separate at this crossroad, you say goodbye with great gratitude for all that the other has been to you, for all the joys and all the pleasures and all the beautiful moments that you have shared with the other. With no misery, with no pain, you simply separate.

Nobody can guarantee that two persons will always be happy together, because people change. When you meet a woman, she is one person, you are one person. After ten years, you will be another person, she will be another person. It is like a river: the water is continuously flowing. The people who had fallen in love are no longer there, both are no longer there. Now you can go on clinging to a certain promise given by somebody else—but *you* had not given it.

A real man of understanding never promises for tomorrow, he can only say, 'For the moment.' A really sincere man cannot promise at all. How can he promise? Who knows about tomorrow? Tomorrow may come, may not come. Tomorrow may come, 'I will not be the same, you will not be the same.' Tomorrow may come, 'You may find somebody with whom you fit more deeply, I may find somebody whom I go with more harmoniously.' The world is vast. Why exhaust it today? Keep doors open, keep alternatives open.

I am against marriage. It is marriage that creates problems. It is marriage that has become very ugly. The most ugly institution in the world is marriage, because it forces people to be phony: they have changed, but they go on pretending that they are the same.

One old man, eighty years old, was celebrating his fiftieth wedding anniversary with his wife who was seventy-five. They went to the same hotel, to the same hill station where they had gone on their honeymoon. The nostalgia! Now he is eighty, she is seventy-five. They booked into the same hotel and took the same room as last time. They were trying to live again those beautiful days of fifty years ago.

When they were going to sleep, the woman said, 'Have you forgotten? Aren't you going to kiss me the way you kissed me on our honeymoon night?'

The old man said, 'Okay,' and got up.

The woman asked, 'Where are you going?'

He said, 'I am going to get my teeth from the bathroom.'

Everything has changed. Now this kiss without teeth or with false teeth is not going to be the same kiss. But the man says, 'Okay.' The journey must have been tiring, and for an eighty-year-old . . . . But people go on behaving as if they were the same.

Very few people really grow up; even if they become aged, they don't grow up. Growing old is not growing up. Real maturity comes through meditation.

Learn to be silent, peaceful, still. Learn to be a no-mind. That has to be the beginning. Nothing can be done before that and everything becomes easier after that. When you find yourself utterly happy and blissful, then even if World War III happens and the whole world disappears leaving you alone, it won't affect you. You will be still sitting under your tree doing *vipassana*.

The day that moment comes in your life, you can share your joy. Now you are able to give love. Before that it is going to be misery, hopes and frustrations, desires and failures, dreams . . . and then dust in your hand and in your mouth. Beware, don't waste time. The earlier you become attuned to no-mind, the better it is. Then many things can flower in you: love, creativity, spontaneity, joy, prayer, gratitude, God.

18

The Playboy

I am in a jam: I love three women. This is hell, and this has been going on for three months. Now what should I do?

YOU MUST BE something of a man! One woman is enough. You need legal protection! But if you have tolerated it patiently for three months, wait a little more. Time settles everything. And women are always more perceptive than men—if you cannot do anything, they are bound to do something.

John and Mary began making love in a railway cutting. As their lovemaking progressed, they rolled down on to the railway tracks in the path of the oncoming express.

The driver, seeing the two bodies ahead on the line, halted the train just in time. Now, delaying the train is a serious offence, and at the trial, the judge demanded an explanation.

'Now look, John,' he said, 'I am a man of the world and I can understand you and your girlfriend having a little fun. But why didn't you get out of the way of the train?'

'Well, it's like this, Your Honour,' said John. 'I was coming, the train was coming and Mary was coming, and I thought that whoever could stop would stop.'

✳

Is this a blessing? After being alone for a long time, I fell in love with three women at the same time, which was easy in the beginning. But as soon as I started to get into a deeper relationship with one, either I ran to the next one, or she wanted to be with someone else. Of course the same happened again as soon as I got in tune with one of the other women. So joy and suffering are pretty close together, but I wonder—am I avoiding something?

Don't you think three are more than enough? Do you think you are avoiding the fourth? One woman is enough to create hell, and you are asking me, '*Is this a blessing?*' It must be a curse in disguise.

'What has happened to Jack? I have not seen him for ages.'
      'Oh, he married the girl he rescued from drowning.'
      'And is he happy?'
      'You bet! But he hates water now.'

You must be a great soul—either so unconscious that even three women cannot create any trouble for you, or so enlightened that 'Who cares?'

While riding home from work one evening, three commuters became friendly in the club car and, after the third round, they began to brag about the relative merits of their respective marital relationships.

The first proudly proclaimed, 'My wife meets my train every evening and we've been married for ten years.'

'That's nothing,' scoffed the second. 'My wife meets me every evening, too, and we've been married for seventeen years.'

'Well, I have got you both beat, fellows,' said the third commuter, who was obviously the youngest in the group.

'How do you figure that?' the first fellow wanted to know.

'I suppose you have got a wife who meets you every evening, too!' sneered the second.

'That's right,' said the third commuter, 'and I'm not even married.'

Three women, and you are not even married! They will make a football of you. And you are asking, '*Is this a blessing*?'—with a question mark of course. Be a little more careful: this is a dangerous place for people like you. There are so many women here and, if you go on like this, soon nothing will be left of you and I will unnecessarily lose a disciple. Think of me too.

Weinstein, a very wealthy businessman, had an unattractive daughter. He found a young man to marry her and after ten years they had two children.

Weinstein called his son-in-law into the office one day. 'Listen,' he said, 'you have given me two beautiful grandchildren, you have made me very happy. I am gonna give you 49 per cent of the business.'

'Thank you, Pop!'

'Is there anything else I could do for you?'

'Yeah, buy me out!'

I am ready to buy you out whatsoever the price. You just inquire of the three women!

Love is significant, a good learning situation, but only a learning situation. One school is enough, three schools are too many. And with three women, you will not be able to learn much, you will be in such a turmoil. It is better to be with one so that you can be more totally one with her, so that you can understand her and your own longings more clearly, so you are less clouded, less in anguish— because love in the beginning is only an unconscious phenomenon. It is biological, it is nothing very precious. Only when you bring your awareness to it, when you become more and more meditative about it, does it start becoming precious, it starts soaring high.

Intimacy with one woman or one man is better than having many superficial relationships. Love is not a seasonal flower, it takes years to grow. And only when it grows does it go beyond biology, and start having something of the spiritual in it. Just being with many women or many men will keep you superficial—entertained maybe, but superficial; occupied certainly, but that occupation is not going to help in inward growth.

But a one-to-one relationship, a sustained relationship so that you can understand each other more closely, is tremendously beneficial. Why is it so? And what is the need to understand the woman or the man? The need is because every man has a feminine part in his being, and every woman has a masculine part in her being. The only way to understand it, the easiest way to understand it, the most natural way to understand it is to be in deep, intimate relationship with someone. If you are a man, be in a deep, intimate relationship with a woman. Let trust grow so all barriers dissolve. Come so close to each other that you can look deep into the woman and the woman can look deep into you. Don't be dishonest with each other.

And if you have so many relationships, you will be dishonest, you will be lying continually. You will have to lie, you will have to be insincere, you will have to say things which you don't mean—and they will all suspect. It is very difficult to create trust in a woman if you have some other relationship. It is easy to deceive a man because he lives through the intellect; it is very difficult, almost impossible, to deceive a woman because she lives intuitively. You will not be able to look directly into her eyes; you will be afraid that she may start reading your soul, and so many deceptive things you are hiding, so many dishonesties.

So if you have many relationships, you will not be able to dive deep into the psyche of the woman. And that is the only thing that is needed: to know your own inner feminine part. Relationship becomes a mirror. The woman starts looking into you and starts finding her own masculine part; the man looks into the woman and starts discovering his own femininity. And the more you become aware of your feminine part—the other pole—the more whole you can be, the more integrated you can be. When your inner man and your inner woman have disappeared into each other, have become dissolved into each other, when they are no longer separate, when they have become one integrated whole, you have become an individual. Carl Gustav Jung calls it the process of individuation. He is right, he has chosen the right word for it. And the same happens to a woman.

But playing with many people will keep you superficial, entertained, occupied, but not growing; and the only thing that matters ultimately is growth, growth of integration, individuality, growth of a centre in you. And that growth needs that you should know your other part. The easiest approach is to know the woman on the outside first, so that you can know the woman inside.

Just like a mirror—the mirror reflects your face, it shows you your face—the woman becomes your mirror, the man becomes your mirror. The other reflects your face, but if you have so many mirrors around you and run from one mirror to another and deceive each mirror about the other, you will be in a chaos, you will go nuts.

You fall in love with a woman because she is so new: the physiology, the proportions of her body, the face, the eyes, the eyebrows, the colour of her hair, the way she walks, the way she turns, the way she says hello, the way she looks. Everything is new, the whole territory unknown: you would like to investigate this territory. It is inviting, it is very inviting; you are caught, hypnotized. And when you start approaching, she starts to run away; that is part of the game. The more she runs, the more enchanting she becomes. If she simply says, 'Yes, I am ready,' half of the enthusiasm will be dead that very moment. In fact, you will start thinking how to run away. So, she gives you a chance to chase her. People are never as happy as while the courting continues—very happy—because it is a chase. Man is basically a hunter, so when the woman is chased, running away, trying to hide here and there, avoiding, saying no, the man gets more and more hot. The challenge becomes intense; the woman has to be conquered. Now he is ready to die for her, or do whatsoever is needed, but the woman has to be conquered. He has to prove that he is no ordinary man.

But once they are married, then everything . . . because the whole interest was in the chase, the whole interest was in the unfamiliar, the whole interest was that the woman was apparently unconquerable. But now she is conquered; now how can that old interest remain? At the most, one can pretend, but the old interest cannot remain. Things start becoming cold. They start getting bored with each other because now there are other women who are again new territories: they attract, they invoke, they call forth.

The same happens with thoughts: you are enchanted with one sort of thinking, but by the time you become acquainted with it, the honeymoon is over, the love is over. Now you would like to be interested in something else, something new that again gives you a thrill, a kick.

This way one goes from one woman to another, from one man to another. This sort of searching will never allow you time enough to create trust.

PART 3

I am useless;
I can only sing,
And my songs are purposeless.

—Rabindranath T

PART

19

The Politician

I am a radical revolutionary politician. Have you something to say to me?

YOU HAVE ALREADY gone too far—you will not listen. Just to be a politician is enough, but you are a revolutionary radical politician—cancer doubled, trebled! Is not politics enough? Have you to be radical, revolutionary? But we always find beautiful words to hide ugly realities.

No politician can be a revolutionary, because the only revolution is spiritual. No politician can be radical either; the very word *radical* means concerning the roots. The politician only prunes the leaves, he has nothing to do with the roots. Only enlightenment takes you to the roots, only meditation takes you to the roots of the problems.

Politics has always existed, politicians have always existed, but what has happened? The world remains the same sorry-go-round! In fact, misery goes on becoming multiplied every day. All these revolutionaries and radical politicians have only proved to be mischievous—with good intentions, of course, but intentions don't count at all. What counts is consciousness.

The politician has no consciousness; in fact, he is

trying to avoid his inner problems, he is trying to escape from his own problems. And the easiest way to do so is to become concerned about world problems, economics, politics, history, service to the poor, transformation of the conditions of society, reformation. All these are strategies for escaping from one's own problems—subtle strategies, dangerous, because one feels that one is doing something great, while one is simply being a coward.

First, face your own problems, encounter them. First try to transform *your* being. Only a transformed person can trigger the processes of transformation in others.

You ask me: '*Have you something to say to me?*' Remember two things. First, the three rules of ruination. There are three ways to be ruined in this world: first is by sex, second is by gambling, and the third is by politics. Sex is the most fun, gambling the most exciting, and politics the surest. Second, remember the fundamental law of all revolutions: when the revolution comes, things will be different—not better, just different.

Politicians have been driving the whole world for centuries—to where, to what end? Is it not time enough that we should see the whole stupidity of the game? At least we are aware, fully aware, of 5,000 years of politics; before that the case must have been the same, but after 5,000 years of political games, what has happened? Man remains in the same darkness, in the same misery, in the same hell. Yes, politics goes on giving him hope—a hope for a better tomorrow, which never comes. Tomorrows never come.

It is the opium of the people. Karl Marx says religion is the opium of the people. It is true, 99.9 per cent it is true; just point 1 per cent it is not true. A Buddha, a Jesus, a Lao Tzu, a Zarathustra—just these few people can be counted in that point 1 per cent, otherwise Karl Marx is

99.9 per cent right, that religion has proved to be the opium of the people. It has kept people in a drugged state, in such a sleep that they can tolerate an intolerable existence, that they can tolerate all kinds of slavery, starvation, in the hope of a better tomorrow. Religions used to give this better tomorrow in the other world, after death.

People come to me and ask, 'What will happen after death?' I don't answer them, I ask them another question instead. I ask them, 'Forget all about after death, let me ask you one thing: what is happening *before* death?' ... because whatsoever is happening before death will continue to happen after death. It is a continuum: your consciousness will be the same, before or after will not make any difference. The body may not be the same, the container may change, but the content will remain the same. Whatsoever happens is happening to the content, not to the container.

First, religion was giving opium to the people—'tomorrow,' 'after death.' Millions of people remained in that state of druggedness, under that chloroform—religious chloroform. Now politics is doing the same. Even communism has proved nothing but a new opium for the masses—communism is a new kind of religion. The strategy is the same: 'Tomorrow will come the revolution, and everything will be all right.' You have to sacrifice your today for tomorrow, and tomorrow never comes.

Eighty years have passed since the Russian Revolution, and tomorrow is still as far away as before. Fifty years have passed since the Indian Revolution, the Gandhian Revolution, and tomorrow remains as far away, in fact, farther away than before. The people who sacrificed, sacrificed in vain; it would have been better if they had lived. The people who were killed were really committing suicide, hoping that they were doing great service to humanity.

Don't create more madness in the world—it is already full of madness.

A colleague of mine once worked in a mental hospital. While making the rounds, he would test the patient by asking, 'Why are you here?' The response usually revealed the patient's degree of reality orientation.

One morning the psychologist received a response that rocked him. 'I am here,' replied the patient, 'for the same reason you are, doc. I couldn't make a go of it in the outside world.'

Patients and doctors, people and politicians are all in the same boat. They are all Ayatollah Khomaniacs! All kinds of maniacs are loose in the world. If you drop out of your radical revolutionary politics, there will be at least one Khomaniac less and that will be a great blessing.

20

The Priest

A YOUNG DEVIL comes running to his boss. He is trembling and says to the old devil, 'Something has to be done immediately, because on earth one man has found the truth! And once people know the truth, what will happen to our profession?'

The old man laughed, and said, 'Sit down and rest and don't be worried. Everything is taken care of. Our people have reached there.'

'But,' he said, 'I have *come* from there: I didn't see a single devil there.'

The old man said, 'The *priests* are my people! They have already surrounded the man who has found the truth. Now they will become the mediators between the man of truth and the masses. They will raise temples, they will write scriptures, they will interpret and distort everything. They will ask people to worship, to pray. And in all this hubbub, the truth will be lost! This is my old method, which has always succeeded.'

The priests, who represent religion, are not its friends. They are the greatest enemies of it, because religion needs no mediators: between you and existence there is an immediate relatedness. All that you have to learn is how to understand the language of existence. You know the languages of man, but they are not the languages of existence.

Existence knows only one language: and that is of silence.

If you can also be silent, you will be able to understand the truth, the meaning of life, the significance of all that exists. And there is no one who can interpret it for you. Everyone has to find it for himself, nobody can do the job on your behalf. But that's what the priests have been doing for centuries. They are standing like a China Wall between you and existence.

Just a few days ago in the Vatican, the pope informed all the Catholics, 'It is being told to me again and again that many Catholics are confessing to God *directly*. They are not going to the confession booth, to the priest. I declare it a sin to confess directly to God. You have to confess to the priest; you cannot relate to God directly.' He has not given any reason, because there is no reason at all, except that the priest has to be kept in his profession—and he himself is a high priest.

If people start approaching reality without anybody leading them, without anybody telling them what is good and what is evil, without anybody giving them a map that they have to follow, millions of people will be able to understand existence—because our heartbeat is also the heartbeat of the universe, our life is part of the life of the total. We are not strangers, we are not coming from somewhere else; we are growing within existence. We are part of it, an essential part of it. We just have to be silent enough so that we can hear that which cannot be said in words: the music of existence, the immense joy of existence, the constant celebration of existence. Once it starts penetrating our heart, transformation comes.

That is the only way somebody becomes religious—not by going to churches, which are made by man, not by reading scriptures, which are made by man. But priests have been pretending that their holy scriptures are written by God. The very idea is simply idiotic! Just look into those scriptures: you will not find any signature of God in them. You will find things which there is no reason for God to write.

Hindus believe in the *Vedas* and believe that they are written by God himself—they are the most ancient books in existence but no Hindu bothers to look into them. If God wrote them, there is going to be something immensely valuable, but 98 per cent of the Vedas are just rubbish—such rubbish that it proves that they are not written by God.

For example, a prayer by a priest . . . why should God write it? And the prayer is that his cows are not giving enough milk, 'Have mercy on me, increase the milk of my cows.' Not only that, '*Decrease* the milk of everybody else's!'—God is going to write this? 'Kill my enemies and help my friends' . . . and even such stupid things as 'Rains are coming; take care that all the water reaches my fields and avoids the neighbouring field because it belongs to my enemy. Just shower your water on *my* field.'

Why should God write these things? Every scripture gives intrinsic evidence that they are written by men, and very stupid men, primitive men. The so-called holy scriptures are not even to be regarded as good literature—they are childish, crude, ugly—but because they are written in languages which are dead . . . . And some are in languages which have never been in use by common people, for example, the *Vedas*. That language has never been used by the common people; it was the language of the learned brahmins, the language of the priests. And they were very reluctant that it be translated, because they knew: once it is translated, it will lose all sanctity. People will see that this nonsense is not even unholy, what to say about its being holy!

So much obscenity, so much pornography is in the holy scriptures of all your religions. But they are written in Sanskrit, which is not used by common people; in Arabic, which is not used by common people; in Hebrew, which is not used by common people; in Pali, in Prakrit . . . . Those languages are dead. And all the religions are reluctant to have their holy scriptures brought in to the modern languages which people understand—although, in spite of their reluctance, their holy scriptures *have* been translated.

First they were against their being printed; second they were against their being translated. The only reason was, they knew that once they were printed, they would be sold all over the world, anybody could purchase them. And if they are translated into living languages, how long can you hide the truth? And how are you going to prove that they are written by God? The scriptures are man-made, the statues of God are man-made, the temples and churches are man-made, but thousands of years of conditioning has given them a certain sacredness, holiness. And there is nothing sacred in them, nothing holy in them.

The priests, more than anybody else, have been deceiving man. This is the worst profession in the world, even worse than the profession of prostitutes. At least the prostitute gives you something in return; the priest gives you simply hot air—he has nothing to give to you.

And this is not all: whenever somebody has realized the truth, these priests are against him. Obviously, they have to be, because if his truth is recognized by people, millions of priests in the world will be out of employment

And their employment is absolutely unproductive. They are parasites, they go on sucking the blood of man. From the moment the child is born, until he enters his grave, the priest goes on finding ways to exploit him.

Unless religion is freed from the hands of priests, the world will remain only with pseudo-religion; it will never become religious. And a religious world cannot be so miserable: the religious world should be a constant celebration.

A religious man is nothing but pure ecstasy. His heart is full of songs. His whole being is ready to dance any moment. But the priest has taken away the search for truth: he says there is no need for searching, it has already been found, you just have to have faith.

The priest has made people miserable, because he condemns all the pleasures of the world. He condemns the pleasures of the world so that he can praise the pleasures of the other world. The other world is his fiction. And he wants humanity to sacrifice its reality for a fictitious idea—and people have sacrificed it.

21

The Scientist

*I heard you say sometime ago that science is of the
head and religion is of the heart. I understand that
these qualities, being of a polarity, are mutually
dependent. One cannot exist without the other,
just as man cannot exist without both head and
heart. Would not then a world scientific community
bring with it, as a necessary by-product, a world
religious community? Is not the vision of a world
science and a world religion synthesized in your
vision of the New Man?*

MAN IS NOT only head and heart. There is something more
than both in him—his being. So you have to understand
three things: the head, the heart and the being.

I have said religion is of the heart, because religion is
the bridge between head and being. The head cannot jump
to the being directly unless it goes through the heart.

Science is confined to the head, reason, logic. The
heart is confined to feelings, emotions, sensitivities. But the
being is beyond both. It is pure silence—no thinking, no
feeling. And only the man who knows his being is
authentically religious. The heart is only a stopover.

But you have to understand my difficulty. You are in the head. I cannot talk about the being because the head will not be able to communicate with the being. For the head, there is no being; that's why scientists go on denying the soul. So I have to talk to you about the heart, which is midway.

It is possible for the head to understand a little bit of the heart, because even the greatest scientist falls in love. His head cannot conceive what is happening—falling in love? He cannot prove it rationally, he cannot find why it happened with a particular man or with a particular woman, what is the chemistry behind it, what is the physics behind it; it seems to be something out of nowhere. But he cannot deny it either; it is there, and it is possessing his whole life. That's why I say religion is of the heart. That is only a temporary statement.

Once I can persuade you to move from thinking into feeling, then I can tell you that religion is of the being. Religion is neither thinking nor feeling, it is neither logic nor emotion. It is just pure silence: in one sense, utterly empty, because there is no feeling, no thinking and, in another sense, overflowing with bliss, with benediction.

Meditation is the way from the head to the heart, from the heart to the being.

I would like all scientists to listen to the heart. That would change the very character of science. It wouldn't be in the service of death, it wouldn't create more and more destructive weapons. It would be in the service of life. It would create better roses, more fragrant roses; it would create better plants, better animals, better birds, better human beings. But the ultimate goal is to move from feeling to being. And if a scientist is capable of using the head as far as the objective world is concerned, using his heart as far as the interpersonal world is concerned, and using his being as far as existence itself is concerned, then he is a perfect man.

My vision of the new man is of a perfect man: perfect in the sense that all his three dimensions are functioning without contradicting each other but, on the contrary, complementing each other.

The perfect man will create a perfect world. The perfect man will create a world of scientists, a world of poets, a world of meditators.

My approach is that all these three centres should be functioning in every person, because even a single individual is a world unto himself. And these centres are in the individual, not in society; hence, my focus is on the person. If I can change the individual, sooner or later the world is to follow. It will *have* to follow, because it will see the beauty of the new man.

The new man is not only clever in arithmetic, he can also enjoy and compose music. He can dance, he can play the guitar—which is tremendous relaxation for his head, because the head is no longer functioning. And the new man is not only of the heart; there are moments when he drops even deeper and simply is. That source of your is-ness is the very centre of your life. To touch it, to be there is to be rejuvenated. All the energies of your heart and of your head will be tremendously multiplied because you will be getting newer energy every day, every moment.

Right now, even a great scientist like Albert Einstein uses only 15 per cent of his potential. What can one say about ordinary people? They never go beyond 5 to 7 per cent. If all the three centres are functioning together, man will be able to function totally, 100 per cent. We can create a paradise here, on this earth. It is within our hands. Just a little effort, a little courage, and nothing more is needed.

The world has to be scientific for all technologies, for all comforts. The world has to be poetic; otherwise man becomes just a robot. The head is a computer. Without poetry and music and dance and song, what your head does can be done by a computer far more efficiently and infallibly. Popes have been declaring that they are infallible. They are not. But if they want to be infallible, their brains can be replaced by a computer; then they will be infallible.

The heart is a totally different dimension—of experiencing beauty, love, and expressing it. But that is not all. Unless you reach to your very centre, you will remain discontented. And a discontented man is dangerous because he will do anything to get rid of his discontentment.

The person who knows himself and his centre is the richest. In fact, that's where the kingdom of God is. It is *your* kingdom, there *you* are a god. Deep down, centred in the being, you become an emperor.

22

The Businessman

I am a businessman. Can I also be a meditator?

ONE HAS TO do something in life. Somebody is a carpenter and somebody is a king; somebody is a businessman while somebody is a warrior. These are ways of livelihood, these are ways of getting bread and butter, a shelter. They can't change your inner being. Whether you are a warrior or a businessman does not make any difference: one has chosen one way to earn his livelihood, the other something else.

Meditation is life, not livelihood.

It has nothing to do with what you *do*, it has everything to do with what you *are*. Yes, business should not enter into your being, that is true. If your being also has become businesslike, it is difficult to meditate and impossible to be a *seeker* . . . because if your being has become businesslike, then you have become too calculative. And a calculative person is a cowardly person: he thinks too much, he cannot take any jumps.

Meditation is a jump: from the head to the heart, and ultimately from the heart to the being. You will be going deeper and deeper, where calculations will have to be left behind, where all logic becomes irrelevant. You cannot carry your cleverness there. In fact, cleverness is not true intelligence either; cleverness is a poor substitute for intelligence. People who are not intelligent learn how to be clever. People who are intelligent need not be clever; they are innocent, they need not be cunning. They function out of a state of not-knowing.

If you are a businessman, that's okay. If Jesus can become a meditator and a seeker, and ultimately a christ, a buddha—and he was the son of a carpenter, helping his father, bringing wood, cutting wood. If a carpenter's son can become a buddha, why not you?

Kabir was a weaver. He continued his work for his whole life; even after his enlightenment, he was still weaving. He loved it! Many times his disciples asked him, prayed to him with tears in their eyes, 'You need not work anymore—we are here to take care of you! With so many disciples, why should you go on in your old age spinning and weaving?'

And Kabir would say, 'But do you know for whom I am weaving, for whom I am spinning? For God!—because everyone is now a god to me. It is my way of prayer.' If Kabir can become a buddha and still remain a weaver, why can't you?

But business should not enter into your being. Business should be just an outside thing, just one of the ways of livelihood. When you close your shop, forget all about your business. When you come home, don't carry the shop in your head. When you are home with your wife, with your children, don't be a businessman. That is ugly: that means your being is becoming coloured by your doing. Doing is a superficial thing. The being should remain transcendental to your doing and you should always be capable of putting your doing aside and entering into the world of your being. That's what meditation is all about . . . .

So remain a businessman, but for a few hours forget all about it. I am not here to tell you to escape from your ordinary life. I am here to tell you the ways and means, the alchemy, to transform the ordinary into the extraordinary.

Be a businessman in your shop and don't be a businessman at home. And sometimes for a few hours forget even the home, family, wife and children. For a few hours, just be alone with yourself. Sink deeper and deeper into your own being. Enjoy yourself, love yourself, and slowly, slowly, you will become aware that a great joy is welling up, with no cause from the outside world, uncaused from the outside. It is your own flavour, it is your own flowering. This is meditation.

'Sitting silently, doing nothing, the spring comes and the grass grows by itself.' Sit silently, doing nothing, wait for the spring. It comes, it always comes, and when it comes, the grass grows by itself. You will see great joy arising in you for no reason at all. Then share it, then give it to people! Then your charity will be inner. Then it will not be just a means to attain to some goal; then it will have intrinsic value.

My *sannyas* is nothing but living in the ordinary world, but living in such a way that you are not possessed by it; remaining transcendental, remaining in the world and yet a little above it. That is *sannyas*.

It is not the old *sannyas* in that you have to escape from your wife, children, business, and go to the Himalayas. That kind of thing has not worked at all. Many went to the Himalayas but they carried their stupid minds with them. The Himalayas have not been of any help to them; on the contrary, they have destroyed the beauty of the Himalayas, that's all. How can the Himalayas help you? You can leave the world, but you cannot leave your mind here. The mind will go with you; it is inside you. And wherever you are, the same mind will create the same kind of world around you.

You can leave the world—you will be the same. You will again create the same world because you carry a blueprint in your mind. It is not a question of leaving the world, it is a question of changing the mind, renouncing the mind. That's what meditation is.

23

The American

The esoteric sect known as Bauls celebrated all aspects of life, including the body. We Americans cherish our bodies with health food, aerobics and massage. In spite of the similarity in approach, I don't think our understanding about the body is the same as that of Bauls, is it?

THERE IS A lot of difference, and the difference is not only quantitative, it is qualitative. The modern world, the modern mind, knows only the empty temple. It has completely forgotten about the one who is enshrined in the temple. So we go on worshipping the temple, but the god is forgotten. Not knowing anything about the centre of life, we go on moving and indulging on the periphery.

The American cherishes his body as the body, the Baul worships his body as the shrine of God. The body in itself is nothing. It is luminous because of something that is beyond the body. The glory of the body is not in the body itself; it is a host—the glory is because of the guest. If you forget the guest, it is sheer indulgence. If you remember the guest, loving the body, celebrating the body is part of worship.

The American worship of the body is meaningless. Hence, people go after health food, massage, and in a thousand and one ways they somehow try to create meaning in their lives. But look into their eyes; a great emptiness exists. You can see they have missed. The fragrance is not there, the flower has not flowered. Deep inside they are just desert-like, lost, not knowing what to do. They go on doing many things for the body but it is missing the target.

I have heard an anecdote:

Rosenfeld walked into the house with a grin on his face. 'You will never guess what a bargain I just got,' he told his wife. 'I bought four polyester, steel-belted, radial wide-tread, white-walled, heavy-duty tyres, on sale!'

'Are you nuts?' said Mistress Rosenfeld. 'What did you buy tyres for? You don't even have a car.'

'So,' said Rosenfeld, 'you buy brassieres, don't you?'

If the centre is missing, you can go on decorating the periphery. It may deceive others but it cannot fulfil you. It may even deceive you sometimes, because even one's own lie repeated too many times starts appearing like the truth. But it cannot fulfil you, it cannot give contentment.

The American is trying hard to enjoy life, but there seems to be no rejoicing. The Baul is not trying at all to enjoy life. There is no effort in it, he simply is enjoying it. And he has nothing to enjoy; he is just a beggar on a road, but he has something of the inner, some glow of the unknown surrounds him. His songs are not only songs; something from the beyond descends in them. When he dances, it is not only that his body is moving; something deeper has moved. He's not *trying* to enjoy.

Remember it: whenever you are trying to enjoy or achieve happiness, you will miss. The very effort to achieve happiness is absurd because happiness is *here*, you cannot achieve it. Nothing has to be done about it, you have simply to allow it. It is happening, it is all around you; within, without, only happiness is. Nothing else is real. Watch, look deep into the world, into trees, birds, rocks, rivers, into the stars, moon and sun, into people, animals. Look deep: existence is made out of the stuff of happiness, joy. It is made of bliss. There is nothing to be done about it. Your very doing may be the barrier. Relax and it fulfils you; relax and it rushes into you; relax and it overflows you.

The Baul is relaxed; the American is tense. Tension arises when you are chasing something, relaxation arises when you are allowing something. That's why I say there is a great difference, and the difference is qualitative. It is not a question of quantity—that Bauls have more than Americans, or Americans have less than the Bauls. No, they have nothing of the happiness that the Bauls have; and what the Americans have—the misery, the tension, the anguish, the neurosis—the Bauls don't have. They exist in a totally different dimension.

The dimension of the Baul is here-now; the dimension of the American is somewhere else—then-there, but never here-now. The American is chasing, chasing hard, trying to get something out of life, trying to squeeze life. Nothing comes out of it because that is not the way. You cannot squeeze life, you have to surrender to it. You will not be able to conquer life. You have to be so courageous as to be defeated by life. Defeat is victory there, and the effort to be victorious is going to prove to be nothing but your final, utter failure.

Life cannot be conquered because the part cannot conquer the whole. It is as if a small drop of water is trying to conquer the ocean. Yes, the small drop can fall into an ocean and become the ocean, but it cannot conquer the ocean. In fact, dropping into the ocean, slipping into it is the way to conquer. Dissolve yourself.

Now let me say this: the American is trying to find happiness, hence his being overly concerned with the body. It is almost an obsession. It has gone beyond the limits of concern, it has become obsessive: continuously thinking about the body, doing this and that, and all sorts of things. He is making an effort to have some contact with happiness through the body. That is not possible. The Baul has attained it. He has already seen it inside himself. He looks deep into his body, not through massage, not through Rolfing, not through a sauna. He has looked into it through love and meditation and has found that it is there, the treasure is there. Hence he worships his body; hence he is careful about his body . . . because the body is carrying the divine. Because of this, that has happened inside—that he has become aware—he is happy with his body, he takes care of his body, he loves his body. This love is totally different.

Secondly: the American mind is competitive. It is not necessarily that you are really in love with your body, you may be just competing with others. Because others are doing things, you have to do them. The American mind is the most shallow, ambitious mind that has ever existed in this world. It is the very basic worldly mind. That's why the businessman has become the topmost reality in America. Everything else has faded into the background; the businessman, the man who controls money, is the topmost reality.

Money is the most competitive realm. You need not have culture, you need only have money. You may not know anything about music, anything about poetry. You need not know anything about ancient literature, history, religion, philosophy—no, you need not know. If you have a big bank balance, you are important. That's why I say this is the most shallow mind that has ever existed. And it has turned everything into commerce. This mind is continuously in competition. Even if you purchase a Van Gogh or a Picasso, you don't purchase it for Picasso; you purchase it because the neighbours have purchased it. They have a Picasso painting in their drawing room, so how can you afford not to have it? You have to have it. You may not know anything, you may not know even how to hang it, which side is which . . . because it is difficult to know, as far as a Picasso is concerned, whether the picture is hanging upside-down or right-side up! You may not know at all whether it is authentically a Picasso or not. You may not look at it at all, but because others have it and they are talking about Picasso, you have to show your culture. You simply show your money. So whatsoever is costly becomes significant, whatsoever is costly is thought to be significant.

Money and the neighbours seem to be the only criteria to decide everything: their cars, their houses, their paintings, their decorations. People have saunas in their bathrooms not because they love their bodies, not necessarily, but because it is the 'in' thing—everybody has it. If you don't have it, you look poor. If everybody has a house in the hills, you have to have one. You may not know how to enjoy the hills, you may be simply bored there. Or you may take your TV and your radio there and just listen to the same programme you were listening to at home, and watch the same TV programme as you were watching at home. What difference does it make where you are sitting— in the hills or in your own room? But others have it. A four-car garage is needed; others have it. You may not *need* four cars.

The American mind is continuously competing with others. The Baul is a non-competitor. He is a dropout. He says, 'I am no longer concerned with what others are doing, I am only concerned with what I am. I am not concerned with what others have, I am only concerned with what I have.' Once you see the fact that life can be tremendously blissful without having many things, then who bothers?

Old Luke and his wife were known as the stingiest couple in the valley. Luke died and a few months later his wife lay dying. She called in a neighbour and said weakly, 'Ruthie, bury me in my black silk dress. But before you do, cut the back out and make a new dress out of it. It is good material and I hate to waste it.'

'Couldn't do that!' exclaims Ruthie. 'When you and Luke walk up them golden stairs, what would them angels say if your dress ain't got a back in it?'

'They won't be looking at me,' she said. 'I buried Luke without his pants.'

The concern is always the other—Luke will be without pants, so everybody will be looking at him. The American concern is with the other; the Baul's concern is simply with himself. The Baul is very selfish; he is not worried about you, and he is not worried about anything that you have or anything that you have done. He is not concerned at all with your biography. He lives on this earth as if he were alone. Of course, he has tremendous space all around him—because he lives on this earth as if he were alone. He moves on this earth without being concerned with the opinions of others. He lives his life, he is doing his thing. Of course, he is happy like a child. His happiness is very simple, innocent. It is not manipulated, it is not manufactured. It is very simple, essential, basic, like a child's.

Have you watched a child just running, shouting, dancing for nothing at all?—because he has nothing. If you ask him, 'Why are you so happy?' he will not be able to answer you. He will really think that you are mad. Is there any need for any cause to be happy? He will simply be shocked that the 'why' can be raised. He will shrug his shoulders and will go on his way and start singing and dancing again. The child has nothing. He is not a prime minister yet, he is not a president of the United States, he is not a Rockefeller. He owns nothing—maybe a few shells or a few stones that he has collected on the seashore, that's all.

The Baul's life does not end when life ends; the American's life ends when life ends. When the body ends, the American ends; hence, the American is very afraid of death. Because of the fear of death, the American goes on trying in any way to prolong his life, sometimes to absurd lengths. Now there are many Americans who are just vegetating in hospitals, in mental asylums. They are not living, they are long since dead. They are just managed by the physicians, medicines, modern equipment. Somehow they go on hanging on.

The fear of death is so tremendous: once gone, you are gone forever and nothing will survive—because the American knows only the body and nothing else. If you know only the body, you are going to be very poor. First, you will always be afraid of death, and one who is afraid to die will be afraid to live—because life and death are so together that if you are afraid to die, you will become afraid to live. It is life that brings death, so if you are afraid of death, how can you really love life? The fear will be there. It is life that brings death; you cannot live it totally.

If death ends everything, if that is your idea and understanding, then your life will be a life of rushing, chasing. Because death is coming, you cannot be patient. Hence, the American mania for speed: everything has to be done fast because death is approaching, so try to manage as many more things as possible before you die. Try to stuff your being with as many experiences as possible before you die, because once you are dead, you are dead.

This creates a great meaninglessness and, of course, anguish, anxiety. If there is nothing which is going to survive the body, whatsoever you do cannot be very deep. Then whatsoever you do cannot satisfy you. If death is the end and nothing survives, life cannot have any meaning and significance. Then it is a tale told by an idiot, full of fury and noise, signifying nothing.

So, on the one hand, the American is constantly running from one place to another to somehow grab the experience, somehow not to miss the experience. He is running all around the world, from one town to another, from one country to another, from one hotel to another. He is running from one guru to another, from one church to another, in search, because death is coming. On the one hand, a constant, mad chasing, and, on the other, a deep-down apprehension that everything is useless—because death will end all. So whether you have lived a rich life or a poor life, whether you were intelligent or unintelligent, whether you were a great lover or missed, what difference does it make? Finally death comes, and it equalizes everybody: the wise and the foolish, the sages and the sinners, the enlightened people and the stupid people, all go down into the earth and disappear. So what is the point of it all? Whether it be a Buddha or a Jesus or a Judas; what difference does it make? Jesus dies on the cross, Judas commits suicide the next day—both disappear into the earth.

On the one hand, there is fear that you may miss and others may attain, and, on the other, a deep apprehension that even if you get what you are after, nothing is got. Even if you arrive, you arrive nowhere because death comes and destroys everything.

This is the understanding of the Baul: that there is no need to go anywhere. Even if you go on sitting under a tree as it happened to Buddha . . . God himself came to him. He was not going anywhere, just sitting under his tree. All comes—you just create the capacity. All comes—you just allow it. Life is ready to happen to you. You are creating so many barriers, and the greatest barrier that you can create is chasing. Because of your chasing and running, whenever life comes and knocks at your door, she never finds you there. You are always somewhere else. When life reaches there, you have moved. You were in Kathmandu; when life reaches Kathmandu, you are in Goa. When you are in Goa and life somehow reaches Goa, you are in Pune. And by the time life reaches Pune, you will be in Philadelphia. So, you go on chasing life and life goes on chasing you, and the meeting never happens.

Be . . . just be, and wait, and be patient.

*

A certain mind has come into existence—the American mind. This is something new in the history of humanity. The American mind—and it is for the first time in the whole history of man that such a mind has existed—is the most trained in dealing with the world. American society is the first society in human history which is dominated by the businessman; hence its success. No society has ever been dominated by the businessman. In India, it was the scholar, the brahmin, the professor, the pundit, who dominated. In England, it was the aristocrats . . . as it was in the rest of Europe. In Japan, it was the warriors, the samurai, who dominated. Never before and nowhere else has the businessman dominated.

The American society and culture are based on the mind of the businessman. In fact, it was said that if a German had to say to somebody, 'I am a businessman,' he felt a little awkward. A *businessman*? A German used to feel very good if he could say that he was a professor. Maybe poor, but a professor in a big university. He may be very rich, but a businessman? Then it is nothing . . . a businessman?

Now in America to be a professor is nothing. Just a professor?—poor fellow! Professors are those who have failed, professors are those who cannot be anything else. When you cannot be anything else, you become a professor, in America. But 'businessman' is a prestigious word. If you are a businessman, that's how one should be. The whole society is based on the businessman's mind, hence its success. It is a tremendously successful society, because wherever the businessman enters, he brings success.

The professor is bound to fail. Wherever intellectuals come into power, society is doomed, because they will argue and quarrel and do everything, but they will never do anything which is utilitarian. They will only miss that which is needed. They will talk about great things—and small things are what life consists of. The businessman looks to the small things, to the minutest detail; he is very earthly.

So I know that the very success of the American mind is a barrier in the inner world. In the inner world, a different approach is needed—unearthly, more poetic, more romantic. But this can be changed. One should become very fluid. I'm not saying to destroy this mind. The mind is good if you are working in the world, so let it be there intact; when needed, use it. In the marketplace, use it. In the marketplace, whatsoever I am talking about and whatsoever I am sharing with you is of no use; never use it in the marketplace.

So one has to be very fluid. Use this mind in the marketplace, but when you go to the inner temple, put it aside. Use another kind of mind, which is there also. You have not used it, that's all.

The most important thing that happened to the first man who walked on the moon was that he suddenly forgot that he was an American. Suddenly, the whole earth was one, there were no boundaries, because there is no map on earth. The American continent, the African continent, the Asian continent, this country and that country all disappeared. Not that he made any effort to put all the opposing camps together; there was not even a Soviet Russia or an America, the whole earth was just simply one.

And the first words that were uttered by the American were, 'My beloved earth!' This is transcendence. For a moment he had forgotten all conditionings: 'My beloved earth!' Now the whole earth belonged to him. This is what actually happens in a state of silence: the whole existence is yours and all opposites disappear into each other, supporting, dancing with each other. It becomes an orchestra.

Mind is conditioned from the outside; it can be ruled from the outside. You have to grow into no-mind, only then can you not be ruled from the outside. Only a man of no-mind is a free man, independent. He is neither German, nor Indian, nor English, nor American—he is simply free.

American, Indian, German . . . these are the names of your prisons, these are not your freedom skies. These are not skies to fly in, these are the prisons you live in.

A free man belongs to himself and nobody else. A free man is simply an energy with no name, no form, no race, no nation. The days of nations and races are past, the days of the individual are coming. In a better world, there will be no Germans, no Indians, no Hindus, no Christians— there will be pure individuals, perfectly free, living their life in their own way, not disturbing anybody's life and not allowing anybody to disturb their lives.

A man asked a rabbi, 'Why didn't Jesus choose to be born in twentieth-century America?'

The rabbi shrugged his shoulders and said, 'In America? It would have been impossible. Where can you find a virgin, firstly? And secondly, where will you find three wise men?'

The American is the most alive person on the earth today. He is the most alive person for the simple reason that 'American' is not a race, it is a mixture—a mixture of all races. It is a meeting-place, a meeting-place of all the countries. America has become the richest country for the simple reason that cross-breeding brings out the best in every child. Other races are small ponds breeding amongst themselves; it is as if you are breeding in your own family. The smaller the race, the lower the standard of its intelligence becomes. That's why it is prohibited for brothers to marry their sisters—for the simple reason that the child will be just dumb, he will not have any salt. He will not really be a man, he will be more a banana or a tomato! He will not have any intelligence.

Intelligence comes through cross-breeding. And America is the most fortunate country in that way, because its whole history is only of 300 years and all the world has met there. It is the future of the world; that's how the whole world is going to be. All other countries should learn something—cross-breeding should become the normal thing. Marry somebody as far away as possible from you. But people marry in just the opposite way. They find somebody in the neighbourhood, somebody of the same religion, of the same race, of the same colour. That is destroying humanity.

Now, you can ask animal breeders—they have raised the quality of all kinds of animals. Ask the people who are working on raising the quality of fruits and vegetables; they have raised the quality of fruits and vegetables for the simple reason that they have used cross-breeding. But about man, we are very unscientific and very superstitious.

In America, all these superstitions have broken down. They had to because it was a new country and the whole world converged there. People from every country, from Spain, Portugal, Italy, France, Holland, Poland, England: from everywhere people gathered together there. A totally new kind of human being has been born which is far more intelligent, far more healthy, lives longer, has tremendous capacities for adventure, has courage. And it has created the richest country in the world.

An Indian, an Englishman and an American were walking in a cemetery. 'When you die, who would you like to be placed alongside of?' asked the American of his buddies.

'Mahatma Gandhi,' said the Indian.

'Winston Churchill,' said the Englishman.

'Well,' said the American, 'I would like to be next to Raquel Welch.'

'Wait a minute,' said the Indian, 'she ain't dead yet!'

'I know,' said the American. 'But nor am I!'

Even small children in America show great insight, intelligence, far more than anywhere else.

Jimmy decided it was time to lecture his young son who was something of a screwball.

'Bob,' he said, 'you're getting to be a young man now and I think you ought to take life more seriously. Just think: if I died suddenly, where would you be?'

'I would be here,' replied the kid. 'The question is, where would *you* be?'

I must remind you: the word 'phony' comes from America. It is derived from 'telephone.' When you are talking to someone on the telephone, have you observed the change? The voice is not the same, the tone is not the same, and no one knows whether on the other side there is another American or a ghost.

I have heard:

One great psychoanalyst was treating a super-rich billionaire. Although his fee was beyond the capacity of millions of people, for the super-rich man it was nothing. The rich man continued: a year passed and he would lie down on the psychoanalyst's couch and would say all kinds of absurd things . . . which fill *your* heads too. It is another thing that you keep them within, but in psychoanalysis, you have to bring them out.

The psychoanalyst was getting bored but he could not get rid of the super-rich man because he was getting so much money from him. Finally, he found an American solution to it. He said to the rich man, 'I have so many other patients, and sometimes your session takes three hours, four hours, five hours. You have time, you have money. I have a humble suggestion to make. I will keep a tape recorder which will listen to you. My four or five hours will be saved and at night, when I have time, I can listen to the tape.'

The rich man said, 'Great!'

The next day when the psychoanalyst was entering his office, he saw the rich man coming out. He said, 'So quick? Are you finished?'

He said, 'No, I have also brought my tape recorder. My tape recorder is talking to your tape recorder. Why should I waste five hours? When tape recorders can do it, what is the need of me coming every day?'

This is how, slowly, man becomes more and more mechanical. He says things, he lives a life, but it is all like a robot.

Dale Carnegie, one of America's most famous philosophers—he would not be recognized as a philosopher anywhere else except in America, but his book, *How To Win Friends and Influence People*, has sold second only to the Bible. And it is full of crap! He suggests that every husband, at least three or four times a day, should say to his wife, 'Darling, I love you so much, I cannot live without you. I cannot conceive of myself without you.' Whether you mean it or not does not matter.

Do you see the phoniness? If you are in love, it is so difficult to say 'I love you,' because words fall short. And to repeat three or four times a mechanical routine . . . you don't mean anything, you are just a gramophone record. Perhaps the needle on the record is stuck: 'Darling, I love you.' The darling also answers, and deep inside both *hate* each other: 'This is the woman who has destroyed my freedom. This is the man who has put me into a prison.'

Only one man in the whole history of America has my respect, and that man is Walt Whitman. I don't consider any other American to be of much worth. But Walt Whitman belongs to the giants of world history.

Walt Whitman is perhaps the only man in the whole

history of America who comes very close to being a mystic. Otherwise, the American mind is very superficial. It is bound to be very superficial because it is only 300 years old. It is a child's mind which is curious about everything: it goes on questioning this and that and even before you have answered it, it has moved to another question. It is not very interested in the answer; it is just curious, it wants to know everything simultaneously. It goes from one religion to another religion, from one master to another master. It goes on searching for answers at the farthest end of the world—but everything remains almost like a fashion.

The psychologists have found that in America everything lasts not more than three years. That is the usual limit for any fashion. A certain toothpaste, a certain soap, a certain shampoo, a certain hair conditioner, a certain guru—they all come into the same marketplace. It has been calculated that in America, every person changes his job every three years, changes his wife every three years, changes his town every three years. Three years seems to be long enough: something new is needed . . . .

Walt Whitman seems to be a rare individual to have been born in America. He should have been born somewhere in the East—and he was immensely interested in the East.

Walt Whitman is one of the people who is not understood in America at all—and yet he is the only one America can be proud of.

The less civilized, the more primitive a person is, the more alive. The more you become civilized, the more you become plastic—you become artificial, you become too cultivated, you lose your roots into the earth. You are afraid of the muddy world. You start living away from the world; you start posing as though you are not of the world. The system of Tantra says: To find the real person, you will have to go to the roots.

So Tantra says: Those who are still uncivilized, uneducated, uncultured, they are more alive, they have more vitality. And that's the observation of the modern psychologist too. An Afro-American is more vital than the white American—that is the fear of the white man. He is very afraid of the black man. The fear is that the white American has become very plastic, and the black American is still vital, still down-to-earth.

The conflict between the blacks and the whites in America is not really the conflict between black and white, it is the conflict between the real and the plastic. And the white American is very afraid, basically because he is afraid that if the black American is allowed, he will lose his woman, the white American will lose his woman. The black man is more vital, sexually more vital, more alive; his energy is still wild. And that is one of the greatest fears of civilized people: to lose their women. They know that if more vital people are available, they will not be able to hold on to their women.

Tantra says: In the world of those who are still primitive, there is a possibility of starting to grow. *You* have grown in a wrong direction; they have not grown yet—they can still choose a right direction, they have more potential. And they don't have anything to undo; they can proceed directly.

Is there some ultimate purpose to everything, or is life just an accident? Can it be said that life is evolving into some ultimate goal?

It is very difficult, specially for the Western mind, to understand that life is purposeless. The West has been thinking in terms of purpose, but the East is considering in terms of purposelessness. The East says life is not a business, it is a play, and a play has no purpose really; it is non-purposeful. Or you can say play is its own purpose, to play is enough. Life is not reaching towards some goal, life itself is the goal. It is not evolving into some ultimate; this very moment, here and now, life is ultimate.

The achieving mind will never be blissful, it will always be tense. And whenever something is achieved, the achieving mind will feel frustrated, because now new goals have to be invented. This is happening in America. Many of the goals of the past century have been achieved, so America is in deep frustration. All the goals of the founding fathers who created America and the American Constitution are almost achieved. In America, for the first time in the whole history of mankind, a society has become affluent. Almost everybody is rich. The poor man in America is a rich man in India.

The goals have almost been achieved—now what should one do? Society has become affluent: food is there, shelter is there, everybody has got a car, radio, refrigerator, TV—now what to do? A deep frustration is felt, some other goals are needed, and there seem to *be* no goals. Instead of one car, you can have two cars—a two-car garage has become the goal—or you can have two houses, but that will be achieved within ten years. Whatsoever the goal, it can be achieved. Then the achieving mind feels frustrated. What to do now? It again needs a goal, and you have to invent a goal.

So the whole of American business now depends on inventing goals. Give people goals—that's what advertisements and the whole business of advertising is doing. Create goals, seduce people: 'Now *this* is the goal! You must have this, otherwise life is purposeless!' They start running, because they have an achieving mind. But where does it lead? It leads into more and more neurosis.

Only a non-achieving mind can be at peace. But a non-achieving mind is possible only with the background of a cosmic purposelessness. If the whole existence is purposeless, there is no need for you to be purposeful. Then you can play, you can sing and dance, you can enjoy, you can love and live, and there is no need to create any goal. Here and now, this very moment, the ultimate is present. If you are available, the ultimate can enter you. But you are not here, your mind is somewhere in the future, in some goal.

Life has got no purpose, and this is the beauty of it. If there were some purpose, life would have been mean—just futile. It is not a business, it is a play. In India, we have been calling it *leela*. Leela means a cosmic play . . . as if God is playing. Energy overflowing, not for some purpose, just enjoying itself; just a small child playing—for what purpose? Running after butterflies, collecting coloured stones on the beach, dancing under the sun, running under the trees, collecting flowers—for what purpose? Ask a child. He will look at you as if you are a fool: there is no *need* for purpose.

Your mind has been corrupted. Universities, colleges, education, society, have corrupted you. They have made it a conditioning deep down within you that unless something has a purpose, it is useless—so everything must have a purpose. A child playing has no purpose. At the most, if the child could explain, he would say, 'Because I feel good. Running, I feel more alive. Collecting flowers, I enjoy, it is ecstatic.' But there is no purpose. The very act in itself is beautiful, ecstatic. To be alive is enough, there is no need for any purpose. Why ask for anything else? Can't you be satisfied just by being alive? It is such a phenomenon! Just think of yourself being a stone. You could have been, because many are still stones. Think of yourself being a tree. You must have been somewhere a tree, a bird, an animal, an insect. And then think of yourself being a man—conscious, alert, the peak, the climax of all possibilities. And you are not content with it. You need a purpose, otherwise life is useless.

Your mind has been corrupted by economists, mathematicians, theologians. They have corrupted your mind because they all talk about purpose. They say, 'Do something if something is achieved through it. Don't do anything which leads nowhere.' But I tell you that the more you can enjoy things which are useless, the happier you will be. The more you can enjoy things which are purposeless, the more innocent and blissful you will be.

When you don't need any purpose, you simply celebrate your being. You feel grateful just that you are, just that you breathe. It is such a blessing that you can breathe, are alert, conscious, alive, aflame. Is it not enough? Do you need something to achieve so that you can feel good, so that you can feel valued, so that you can feel life is justified? What more can you achieve than what you are? What more can be added to your life? What more can you add to it? Nothing can be added, and the effort will destroy you—the effort to add something. But for many centuries all over the world they have been teaching every child to be purposive. 'Don't waste your time! Don't waste your life!' And what do they mean? They mean, 'Transform your life into a bank balance. When you die, you must die rich. That is the purpose.'

Here in the East, they say, 'Live richly.' In the West, they say, 'Die a rich man.' And these are totally different things. If you want to *live* richly, you have to live here and now, not a single moment is to be lost. If you want to achieve something, you will die a rich man—but you will live a poor man, your life will be poor.

Look at rich people: their life is absolutely poor because they are wasting it, transforming it into bank balances, changing their life into money, into big houses, big cars. Their whole effort is that life has to be changed for some things. When they die, you can count their things.

A meditator needs a non-achieving mind, but a non-achieving mind is possible only if you can be content with purposelessness. Just try to understand the whole cosmic play and be a part in it. Don't be serious, because a play can never be serious. And even if the play needs you to be serious, be *playfully* serious, don't be really serious. Then this very moment becomes rich. Then this very moment, you can move into the ultimate.

The ultimate is not in the future, it is the present, hidden here and now. So don't ask about purpose—there is none, and I say it is beautiful that there is none. If there were purpose, your God would be just a managing director or a big business man, an industrialist, or something like that.

Why waste time in thinking in terms of business? Why not live more and more playfully, non-seriously, ecstatically? Ecstasy is not something which you can achieve by some efforts, ecstasy is a way of living. Moment to moment, you have to be ecstatic, simple things have to be enjoyed. And life gives millions of opportunities to enjoy. You will miss them if you are purposive.

If you are not purposive, every moment you will have so many opportunities to be ecstatic. A flower, a lonely flower in the garden . . . you can dance if you are non-purposive. The first star in the evening . . . you can sing if you are non-purposive. A beautiful face . . . you can see the divine in it if you are non-purposive. All around the divine is happening, the ultimate is showering. But you will be able to see it only if you are non-purposive and playful.

While touring the west coast on his first visit to the United States, an Englishman strikes up a conversation with an

American. 'I say, you really do have a remarkable country here—lovely women, big cities . . . . But, old chap, if you will permit me to be perfectly frank, the fact is: you have no *aristocracy*.'

'No *what*?' asks the American.

'No aristocracy.'

'What's that?' asks the American, looking blank

'Oh, you know,' the Englishman replies. 'People who never do anything, whose parents never did anything, and whose grandparents never did anything—whose families have always been people of leisure.'

'Oh, yeah!' the American's face lights up with comprehension. 'We have them here, but we call them hoboes!'

Do you know that the more a country becomes educated, the more the number of mad people increases there? America has the highest number of mad people today. It is a matter of pride! It is proof that America is the most educated, the most civilized country. American psychologists say that if the same system continues for another hundred years, it will be difficult to find a sane man in America. Even today, the minds of three out of four people are in a shaky condition.

In America alone, three million people are consulting psychoanalysts every day! Slowly, slowly in America the number of physicians is becoming less and psychoanalysts are increasing. The physicians also say that 80 per cent of man's diseases are of the mind, not of the body. And as the understanding grows, this percentage increases. First they used to say 40 per cent, then they started saying 50 per cent; now they say that 80 per cent of diseases are of the mind, not of the body. And I assure you that after twenty to twenty-five years, they will say that 99 per cent of diseases are of the mind, not of the body. They will have to say so because our whole emphasis is being given to man's brain. The brain has become insane.

A man who gets angry in an ordinary way, just as everybody else does—if you insult him, he gets angry—is not a dangerous person because he will never accumulate so much anger that he can prove dangerous. But a man who goes on repressing his anger is sitting on a volcano; any day, the volcano can erupt. Either he is going to commit suicide or murder—less than that won't do.

It is because of repressive religions that so much pornography exists in the world. Pornography exists because of the priests, not because of the 'Playboys.' In fact, the Playboys are only by-products of the priests. So much pornography exists simply because so much sex has been repressed; it wants to find some way, some outlet. And once you repress sex, it starts finding perverted ways. It can become a political trip—it is sexuality, nothing else, repressed sexuality.

That's why in all the armies of the world, sex is repressed. And American soldiers have been continuously in difficulty for the simple reason that it is the first time that any army has been allowed some sexual outlet. American soldiers cannot win, their defeat is certain. Whatsoever they do, wherever they go, they will be defeated for the simple reason that American soldiers are a new phenomenon in the world—they are not sexually repressive. They can't win against the Russians—they could not even win against the Vietnamese. The poor Vietnamese defeated one of the greatest world powers that has ever existed in the whole history of man for the simple reason that if sex is repressed then a man is very dangerous, really dangerous—he is boiling within. He wants to hit hard, he wants to be violent.

The person who is sexually satisfied is not really interested in killing. In fact, all the surveys of American armies show that at least 30 per cent of the soldiers did not use their weapons in the war. Thirty per cent is a big percentage. And if 30 per cent of soldiers are not using their weapons at all, they simply go every day to the front and come back without killing anybody, how are they going to win? They are not interested in killing, there is no desire to kill.

Killing arises only if sex is very repressed. It is a strange fact that whenever a society has been affluent, rich, sexually free, it was destroyed by poor, backward, repressive societies. That was the fate of Greek civilization, that was the fate of Roman civilization, that was the fate of Hindu civilization, and that is going to be the fate of American culture. It is very strange that the further evolved a society is, the more it is vulnerable to being destroyed easily by the less evolved, because the less evolved are more repressive. They are more foolish, they are more stupid; they still go on listening to the priests.

The scene was the latest Olympic games. In the quarters of the American wrestling team stood John Mack, the trainer, warning his protege, Mike 'Bull' Flamm, about the forthcoming match.

'You know,' Mack said, 'the Georgian wrestler you are about to tackle, Ivan Katruvsky, is one of the greatest wrestlers in the world. But he really is not as good as you are. The only thing he's got that makes him a terror is his pretzel-hold. If he once gets a man in his pretzel-hold, that man is doomed. He has used the pretzel-hold on twenty-seven competitors, and in each case his opponent gave up within ten seconds.

'So, listen to me, Bull, you have got to be damned

careful. Never let him get you in that pretzel-hold. If he once clamps you in it, you're a goner!'

Bull listened carefully to Mack's instructions on how to avoid that crippling grip of Ivan's. For the first three minutes of the bout, neither the American nor the Georgian could gain an advantage. The crowd was on edge. Then, suddenly, pandemonium broke loose—Bull Flamm had fallen into the clutches of Ivan's pretzel-hold and was moaning in agony. Mack knew the match was lost, and he left the arena in deep gloom. Down the corridor, the echoes of Bull's anguished cries still reached him. And then, as Mack was about to enter his quarters, he heard an enormous shout arise from the stadium, a cheer the likes of which he had never heard in all his long experience. The stands were in absolute uproar. From the shouts, Mack knew that Bull had won the match, but he couldn't understand it. What could have caused the unthinkable turnabout?

A minute later, Flamm came trotting into the American dressing room. His trainer threw his arms around him, and said, 'Bull, how in hell did you ever get out of that pretzel-hold?'

'Well,' answered Flamm, 'he twisted me into such shapes that I never felt such agony in my life. I thought my bones were going to break. And as I was just about to faint, I saw two balls hanging in front of me. With one desperate lunge, I bit those balls. Well, Mack, you can't imagine what a man is capable of when he bites his own balls.'

24

The Buddha

MAN IS A seed of great potential: man is the seed of buddhahood. Each man is born to be a buddha. Man is not born to be a slave but to be a master. But there are very few who actualize their potential. And the reason why millions can't realize their potential is that they take it for granted that they already have it.

Life is only an opportunity to grow, to be, to bloom. Life in itself is empty; unless you are creative, you will not be able to fill it with fulfilment. You have a song in your heart to be sung and you have a dance to be danced, but the dance is invisible, and the song—even you have not heard it yet. It is hidden deep down in the innermost core of your being; it has to be brought to the surface, it has to be expressed.

That's what is meant by 'self-actualization'. Rare is the person who transforms his life into a growth, who transforms his life into a long journey of self-actualization, who becomes what he was meant to be. In the East, we have called that man the Buddha, in the West, we have called that man the Christ. The word *christ* exactly means what the word *buddha* means: one who has come home.

We are all wanderers in search of the home, but the

search is very unconscious—groping in the dark, not exactly aware what we are groping for, who we are, where we are going. We go on like driftwood, we go on remaining accidental. And it becomes possible because millions of people around you are in the same boat, and when you see that millions are doing the same things that you are doing, then you must be right—because millions can't be wrong. That is your logic, and that logic is fundamentally erroneous: millions can't be *right*. It is very rare that a person is right; it is very rare that a person realizes the truth. Millions live lives of lies, lives of pretension. Their existences are only superficial; they live on the circumference, utterly unaware of the centre. And the centre contains all: the centre is the kingdom of God.

The first step towards buddhahood, towards the realization of your infinite potential, is to recognize that up to now, you have been wasting your life, that up to now, you have remained utterly unconscious.

Start becoming conscious; that is the only way to arrive. It is arduous, it is hard. To remain accidental is easy; it needs no intelligence, hence it is easy. Any idiot can do it—all the idiots are already doing it. It is easy to be accidental because you never feel responsible for anything that happens. You can always throw the responsibility on to something else: fate, God, society, economic structure, the state, the church, the mother, the father, the parents . . . . You can go on throwing the responsibility on to somebody else; hence it is easy.

To be conscious means to take the entire responsibility on your shoulders. To be responsible is the beginning of buddhahood.

When I use the word *responsible*, I am not using it in the ordinary connotation of being dutiful. I am using it in its real, essential meaning: the capacity to respond—that's my meaning. And the capacity to respond is possible only if you are conscious. If you are fast asleep, how can you respond? If you are asleep, the birds will go on singing but you will not hear them, and though the flowers will go on blooming, you will never be able to sense the beauty, the fragrance, the joy, that they are showering on existence.

To be responsible means to be alert, conscious. To be responsible means to be mindful. Act with as much awareness as you can find possible. Even small things— walking on the street, eating food, taking a bath—should not be done mechanically. Do them with full awareness.

Slowly, slowly, small acts become luminous, and, by and by, those luminous acts go on gathering inside you— finally . . . the explosion. The seed has exploded, the potential has become actual. You are no longer a seed but a lotus flower, a golden lotus flower, a one-thousand petalled lotus flower.

And that is the moment of great benediction; Buddha calls it *nirvana*. One has arrived. Now there is no more to achieve, nowhere to go. You can rest, you can relax—the journey is over. Tremendous joy arises in that moment, great ecstasy is born.

But one has to begin from the beginning.

✳

The West has given birth to Aristotle, Nietzsche, Heidegger, Camus, Berdyaev, Marcel and Sartre. Is it going to give birth to buddhas by itself or is a communion with the Eastern consciousness needed?

The buddha-consciousness is neither Eastern nor Western. It has nothing to do with geography or history, it has nothing to do with mind as such. Mind is Eastern, Western, Indian, Chinese, Japanese, German, but the innermost pure consciousness is simply the pure sky—you cannot identify it with anything because it is unconditioned.

What is East and what is West?—ways of conditioning, different ways of conditioning. What is a Hindu and what is a Jew?—different ways of conditioning. These are names of diseases. Health is neither Eastern nor Western.

A child is born, and immediately the conditioning starts—very subtle are the ways of conditioning. Directly, indirectly, we start pressing the child into a certain mould. He will speak a certain language, and each language has distinct ways of thinking, each language has its emphasis, its particular direction. That's why sometimes it becomes impossible to translate from one language into another; the other language may not even have words which correspond, the other language may not have looked at reality and life in that way. Life is infinite; the way you look at it is finite—there can be infinite ways of looking at it.

And then the child starts getting coloured by the family, by the school, the church, the priest, the parents—and it goes on silently. Slowly, slowly, the whole sky of consciousness is closed; only a small window, an aperture, is left open. That aperture is Indian, English, American. That aperture is Hindu, Jaina, Buddhist. That aperture is Eastern, Western.

To realize Buddhahood is to regain the consciousness that you brought with your birth. That uncontaminated purity, that original face without any masks, that innocence is buddhahood. So buddhahood cannot be Eastern or Western; it is transcendental.

You may be surprised that when a child grows up in a family . . . and each child has to grow in a family. It is almost a must, there is no other way; some kind of family is needed. Even if it is a commune, it will have its own limitations, it may be a kibbutz but it will have its limitations. And there is no way to bring up a child without a certain nourishing surrounding. That nourishing surrounding is a must, without it, the child cannot survive; the child has to be looked after, but the child has to pay for it. It is not simple, it is very complex. The child has to continuously adjust himself to the family because the family is 'right,' the father is 'right,' the mother is 'right.' They are powerful people—the child is helpless. He has to depend on them, he has to look up to them, and he has to follow them. Right or wrong is not the question: the child has to become a shadow, an imitator.

That's what Hinduism is, Christianity is, that's what the Eastern and the Western mind is. And it is very subtle; a child may never become aware of it, because it is not done in one day, it goes on so slowly—just like the water falling from the mountain, falling and falling and falling, and it destroys the rocks, and the stones disappear.

The child has to adjust in many ways. That adjustment makes him false, inauthentic, makes him untrue—untrue to his own being. Now psychologists have discovered that if a certain child proves to be stupid, it may not be so, because no child is born stupid. It may be just the whole surrounding, the family, that he had to adjust to. If the father is too intellectual, the child will have to behave in a stupid way to keep a balance. If the child behaves in an intelligent way, the father is, in a subtle way, angry. He cannot tolerate an intelligent child, he never tolerates anybody who is trying to be more intelligent than him. He will force the child to remain inferior, notwithstanding what he goes on saying. And the child will learn the trick of behaving like a fool, because when he behaves like a fool, everything goes okay, everything is perfectly okay. The father may show his displeasure on the surface, but deep down he is satisfied. He always likes fools around him; surrounded by fools, he is the most intelligent person.

Because of this, over hundreds of years, women have learned a trick: they never try to be intellectual—the husband won't like it. Not that they are not intelligent, they are as intelligent as men—but they have to learn. Have you not watched it? If the wife is more educated, the husband feels a little bad about it. No man wants to marry a woman who is more educated than him, more famous than him. Not only that, but in small things too: if the woman is taller, no man wants to marry her. Maybe it is just because of this that women have decided on a biological level not to become too tall—there may be some kind of psychological reason in it—otherwise you will not get a husband. If you are too intelligent, you will not be married. The woman has to pretend that she always remains a baby, childish, so that the husband can feel good that the woman leans on him.

In a family, the child comes into a ready-made situation. Everything is already there; he has to fit himself into it, he has to adjust to it. He cannot be himself; if he tries to be himself, he always gets into trouble and starts feeling guilty. He has to adjust—whatsoever the cost. Survival is the most important thing, the first thing, other things are secondary. So each child has to adjust to the family, to the parent, to geography, to history, to the idiosyncrasies of people around him, to all kinds of prejudices, stupid beliefs, superstitions. By the time you become aware or you become a little bit independent, you are so conditioned, the conditioning has gone so deep in the blood and the bones and the marrow, that you cannot get out of it.

What is buddhahood ? Buddhahood is getting out of this whole conditioning . . . . A buddha is one who lives as a whole, as an organic whole. Buddha-consciousness is transcendental consciousness. It has nothing to do with East or West.

✳

What are the characteristics of an enlightened being?

An enlightened being simply means a man who has no longer any questions left in his life, everything is solved. An enlightened man means a man who is constantly in the same state of silence, peace and contentment whatsoever happens on the outside: success or failure, pain or pleasure, life or death.

An enlightened man means a man who has experienced something that you are also capable of, but you have not tried it. He is full of light, joy, ecstasy, twenty-four hours a day. He is almost a drunkard, drunk with the divine. His life is a song, his life is a dance, his life is a rejoicing. And his presence is a blessing.

If you want to know him, you have to be with him. You cannot watch him from the outside, you have to come close. You have to come in a state of intimacy. You have to join his caravan, you have to hold his hand, to feed on him, and you have to allow, to let him enter your heart. But from the outside, please don't try to find any characteristic; these are all inner experiences . . . .

But some indications can always be given. In the proximity of the enlightened being, you will feel a certain magnetic force, a tremendous attraction, a charismatic centre. Out of your fear, you may not come close. It is dangerous to come close to an enlightened man, because you can come close, but then you cannot go away. Coming close is risky. It is only for gamblers, not for businessmen.

PART 4

PART 4

25

The New Man

SOMETIME AGO WHEN we visited the Kennedy Space Center, Florida, we saw the ultimate in science to explore outer space and create 'a better man.' Your vision is concerned with creating the 'new man.' The former is the launching pad for the world's richest and most powerful nation. Yours is the flying saucer for the new consciousness, and yet is decried by one of the world's poorest nations. One is matter and the other, spirit. What is happening?

The idea of a better man is an old idea, very old, as old as man himself. Everybody is willing to accept a better man because it needs no radical change. A better man means something is added to you: you remain the same, you remain continuous; there is no discontinuity. And you become richer, better. The idea of a better man is rooted in greed, hence everybody will support it. The rich countries will support it, the poor countries will support it. India was totally in favour of Mahatma Gandhi because he was trying to bring a better man. The idea of a better man is reformatory, it is not revolutionary.

But the idea of a new man is dangerous because it requires guts. Its basic requirement is that you have to die to the old and you have to be born anew—it is a rebirth.

Hence, I am opposed. And it is not only in India that I am opposed and decried, I will be opposed and decried anywhere else in the world. Even if I am in Florida, the same will happen.

In fact, there is more possibility of opposition in a richer and powerful country than there is in a poor and starving country, for the simple reason that millions of Indians have no idea of what is going on here. They have no time, they have no interest. It is not a vital issue for them, the birth of a new man. Their vital problem is how to survive, and you are talking of the birth of a new man! They are not even able to survive. Their problems are totally different. They are ill, they are hungry, their children are uneducated, they are unemployed, they don't have any land, no food, no shelter—and you are talking about a new man? They are not interested; it is not their problem.

But if I talk about the new man in America, I will be killed immediately, imprisoned. I will not be tolerated at all, because that means a danger to the whole American way of life.

The American way of life depends on ambition, and my new man has to be utterly ambitionless. America's whole approach is: things should be bettered, everything should be made better. It does not matter where it is going to lead, but things have to be better, better and better. They are obsessed with the idea of bettering things. You have to have more speed, better machines, better technology, better railroads, better roads—everything better! Of course, in the same way, you need a better man. It fits with the whole American style of life. Man is also thought to be a commodity. Just as you need better cows and better dogs and better cars and better airplanes, you need a better man! There is no difference, it is the same logic.

I am talking about a new man. The new man is not

necessarily the better man. He will be livelier, he will be more joyous, he will be more alert, but who knows whether he will be better or not? As far as politicians are concerned, he will not be better, because he will not be a better soldier—he will not be ready to be a soldier at all. He will not be competitive, and the whole competitive economy will collapse. He will not be interested just in accumulating junk, and the whole economy depends on that. All your advertising agencies are just bringing to your mind the idea of collecting more and more junk.

The new man will have a totally different vision of life. He will live in a more loving way, because to him love is richness. He will know that money cannot buy love or joy. He will know that money is utilitarian; it is not the goal of life.

The whole American system depends on doing better. 'Do it better!' What you are doing is not the point. 'If you are murdering people, do it better!' You can see what happened in Hiroshima and Nagasaki: America really did it in a better way than anybody else has ever done it. 'Reach the moon!' Nobody asks why. If you ask why, you are crazy; such questions are not to be asked. The only question worth asking is: 'How to reach the moon in a better way than anybody else? Defeat Russia. It should be an American who is first to walk on the moon.' For what? That is not the point. As far as I am concerned, I can't see the point. The American standing on the moon looks so silly! But that is their way of thinking, their philosophy: 'Even if you are looking silly, look silly in a better way. Defeat everybody else!'

My new man means the end of the old world. And why is the new man decried? He has always been decried. Jesus was killed because he was talking about the new man, not about the better man. Jesus said to Nicodemus,

'Unless you are born again, you shall not enter into my kingdom of God.' Jesus insisted that first you have to die to the past, only then can a new consciousness arise in you. He was crucified. Socrates was talking about a new man, remember. Why did such cultured people become so animalistic, so barbarous as to kill a man like Socrates? He was talking about the new man. If he had talked about the better man, he would have been worshipped.

Those who have talked about the better man have always been worshipped, because they are telling you that the past is beautiful but it can be beautified more. They are not against the past, they are not against conventions, they are not against traditions; they are all for them. The tradition has to be the foundation and on that foundation, you can raise a better temple, a better house.

To talk about the new man is dangerous. A new man means cutting away totally from the past, disrupting, uprooting yourself completely from the past, dying to the past and living in the present. And old habits die very hard. We have become accustomed to hearing about a better man; it has gone into the very circulation of our blood. Every saint, every mahatma talks about the better man; that's his business, we know. But about a new man? Then we become afraid. He is bringing something absolutely new; he is taking us into the territory of the unknown, he is trying to uproot us from the familiar. And we have lived for thousands of years in a particular way; we are conditioned by it, we are part of it. Only very few people can manage to get out of it. Hence, my message is going to remain only for the chosen few.

Remember, old habits die hard—and our religions, our philosophies are very old, our styles of life are very old. And I am for the new. We think old is gold—and I say old is just junk! I agree with Henry Ford that history is bunk.

It is all bullshit! We have to free man from all that has gone before, and we have to free man totally, absolutely, categorically.

'Mummy, why did you marry daddy?'
'Ah!' replies the mother. 'So you are wondering too!'

'Didn't I meet you in Texas?'
'I've never been to Texas.'
'Neither have I. Guess it must have been two other fellows.'

These drunkards, these unconscious people have been dominating the whole of humanity. Mad people and drunkards—they have been our deciding factors in the past. We have never listened to the awakened ones. The awakened ones cannot talk about bettering man. It is like telling an ill person, 'I will give you medicine to better your illness.' The ill person does not want to better his illness; he wants to get rid of it, he wants to be healthy.

26

The Meditator

I have heard meditation sometimes described as a science, and at other times as an art; on occasion, you have even called it a knack. Please explain.

MEDITATION IS SUCH a mystery that it can be called a science, an art, a knack, without any contradiction.

From one point of view, it is a science because there is a clear-cut technique that has to be done. There are no exceptions to it, it is almost like a scientific law. But from a different point of view, it can also be said to be an art. Science is an extension of the mind—it is mathematics, it is logic, it is rational.

Meditation belongs to the heart, not to the mind—it is not logic; it is closer to love.

It is not like other scientific activities, but more like music, poetry, painting, dancing; hence, it can be called an art. But meditation is such a great mystery that calling it 'science' and 'art' does not exhaust it. It is a knack—either you get it or you don't get it. A knack is not a science, it cannot be taught. A knack is not an art. A knack is the most mysterious thing in human understanding.

For example, you may have come across people . . . .

Somebody has the knack of becoming a friend immediately. Just meeting him in the bus for a few moments and you suddenly feel as if you have known each other forever, perhaps for many lives. And you cannot pinpoint what is going on, because you have just seen the man for the first time . . . A knack is something mysterious, just a few people can do it.

I know a man who can make his ear lobes move! I have not found another person who can move his ear lobes. Now what do you call it?—a science or what? Because I have asked doctors, 'What do you say about ear lobes moving?' They say, 'It is impossible.' But I brought my friend to one doctor and I told him, 'Show this doctor . . . .' The doctor said, 'My God! He moves his ear lobes very easily, without any trouble.'

In fact, ear lobes have no biological possibility of movement, you have no control over them. You try: you don't have any control. They are *your* ear lobes, but still you have no control over them. But I know one man who manages it. I have asked him, 'How do you manage?' He said, 'I don't know. Just, from the very beginning, I have been doing it.' It is absolutely impossible, physically impossible—because to move those lobes, you need a certain nervous system to control them, and the nerve system is not there. The lobe is just flesh.

Meditation, in the last resort, is a knack too.

That's why for thousands of years people have been meditating, teaching, but very few people have achieved heights in meditation, and very few people have even tried. The vast majority of humanity has not even bothered to think about it. It is something . . . a seed you are born with. If you don't have the seed, a master can go on showering all his bliss on you, still nothing will happen in you. And if the seed is there, just the presence of the master, just the way he looks into your eyes—and something of tremendous importance happens in you, a revolution that you cannot explain to anybody.

It is one of the difficulties for all meditators that they cannot explain to their friends, their families, what they are doing . . . because the majority of humanity is not interested in it at all. And those who are not interested in it at all simply think about people who are interested that something is loose in their heads, something is wrong.

'Sitting silently, doing nothing, the spring comes and the grass grows by itself'—but in the first place, why should you bother about the grass? Basho's beautiful *haiku* will look absurd to them. Grass will grow by itself whether you sit silently or not! Why waste your time?—the grass is going to grow by itself. Let the spring come— spring comes by itself, grass grows by itself. Why are you wasting your time? Do something else meanwhile.

If a man has not something in his heart already—a small seed—then it is impossible for him. He can learn the technique, he can learn the art. But if the knack is missing, he is not going to succeed. So thousands of people start meditation, but very few—so few that they can be counted on ten fingers—ever achieve enlightenment. And unless meditation becomes enlightenment, you have simply wasted your time.

❋

What are the indications that one's meditativeness is going deeper?

Really, there are no milestones—because there is no fixed road. And everyone is on a different road, we are not on one road. Even if you are following one technique of meditation, you are not on the same road; you cannot be.

There is no public path. Every path is individual and personal. So no one's experiences on the path will be helpful to you; rather, they may be damaging.

Someone may be seeing something on his path. If he tells you that this is the sign of progress, you may not meet the same sign on your path. The same trees may not be on your path, the same stones may not be on your path. So do not be a victim of all this nonsense. Only certain inner feelings are relevant. For example, if you are progressing, certain things will begin to happen spontaneously. One, you will feel more and more contentment.

Really, when meditation is completely fulfilled, one becomes so contented that he forgets to meditate—because meditation is an effort, a discontent. If one day you forget to meditate and you do not feel any addiction, you do not feel any gap, you are as fulfilled as ever, then know it is a good sign. There are many who will do meditation, and then if they are not doing it, a strange phenomenon happens to them. If they do it, they do not feel anything. If they do not do it, then they feel the gap. If they do it, nothing happens to them. If they do not do it, then they feel that something is missing.

This is just a habit. Like smoking, drinking, like anything, this is just a habit. Do not make meditation a habit. Let it be alive! Then discontent will disappear by and by; you will feel contentment. And not only while you are meditating. If something happens only while you are meditating, it is false, it is hypnosis. It does some good, but it is not going to be very deep. It is good only in comparison. If there is nothing happening, no meditation, no blissful moment, do not worry about it. If something is happening, do not cling to it. If meditation is going rightly, deep, you will feel transformed throughout the whole day. A subtle contentment will be present every moment. With whatsoever you are doing, you will feel a cool centre inside—contentment.

Of course, there will be results. Anger will be less and less possible. It will go on disappearing. Why? Because anger shows a non-meditative mind—a mind that is not at ease with itself. That is why you get angry with others: basically, you are angry with yourself. Because you are angry with yourself, you go on getting angry with others.

Have you observed that you get angry only with those people who are very intimate with you? The more the intimacy, the more the anger. Why? The greater the gap between you and the person, the less the anger that will be there. You do not get angry with a stranger. You get angry with your wife, with your husband, with your son, with your daughter, with your mother. Why? Why do you get more angry with persons who are more intimate with you? The reason is this: you are angry with yourself. The more intimate a person is with you, the more he has become identified with you. You are angry with yourself, so whenever someone is near you, you can throw your anger upon him. He has become part of you.

With meditation, you will be more and more happy with yourself—remember, with yourself.

It is a miracle when someone becomes happier with himself. For us, either we are happy with someone or angry with someone. When one becomes happier with oneself—this is *really* falling in love with oneself. And when you are in love with yourself, it is difficult to be angry. The whole thing becomes absurd. Less and less anger will be there, more and more love, and more compassion. These will be signs—the general signs.

So do not think you are achieving much if you are beginning to see light or if you go on seeing beautiful colours. They are good, but do not feel satisfied unless real psychological changes are there: less anger, more love; less cruelty, more compassion. Unless this happens, your seeing lights and colours and hearing sounds are child's play. They are beautiful, very beautiful; it is good to play with them—but that is not the aim of meditation. They happen on the road, they are just by-products, but do not be concerned.

Many people will come to me and they will say, 'Now I am seeing a blue light, so what does this sign mean? How much have I progressed?' A blue light will not do because your anger is giving a red light. Basic psychological changes are meaningful, so do not go for toys. These are toys, spiritual toys. These things are not the ends.

In a relationship, observe what is happening. How are you behaving towards your wife now? Observe it. Is there any change? That change is meaningful. How are you behaving with your servant? Is there any change? That change is significant. And if there is no change, then throw away your blue light—it is of no help. You are deceiving and you can go on deceiving. These are easily achieved tricks.

That is why a so-called religious man begins to feel himself religious: because now he is seeing this and that. But he remains the same; he even becomes worse! Your progress must be observed in your relationships. Relationship is the mirror: see your face there. Always remember that relationship is the mirror. If your meditation is going deep, your relationships will become different— totally different! Love will be the basic note of your relationships, not violence. As it is, violence is the basic note. Even if you look at someone, you look in a violent way. But you are accustomed to it.

Meditation for me is not a child's play, it is a deep transformation. How can one know this transformation? It is being reflected every moment in your relationships. Do you try to possess someone? Then you are violent. How can one possess anyone? Are you trying to dominate someone? Then you are violent. How can one control anyone? Love cannot dominate, love cannot possess.

So whatsoever you are doing, be aware, observe it, and then go on meditating. Soon you will begin to feel the change. Now there is no possessiveness in relationships. By and by, possessiveness disappears, and when possessiveness is not there, relationship has a beauty of its own. When possessiveness is there, everything becomes dirty, ugly, inhuman. But we are such deceivers that we will not look at ourselves in relationships—because there the real face can be seen. So we close our eyes to our relationships and go on thinking that something is going to be seen inside.

You cannot see anything inside. First you will feel your inner transformation in your outer relationships, and then you will go deep. Then only will you begin to feel something inner. So probe, penetrate into your relationships, and look there to see whether your meditation is progressing or not.

If you feel a growing love, unconditional love, if you feel a compassion without cause, if you feel a deep concern for everyone's welfare, well-being, your meditation is growing. Then forget all other things. With this observation, you will also observe many things in yourself. You will be more silent, less noise within. When there is need, you will talk, when there is no need, you will be silent. As the case is now, you cannot be silent within. You will feel more at ease, relaxed. Whatsoever you are doing, it will be a relaxed effort; there will be no strain. You will become less and less ambitious. Ultimately, there will be no ambition. Even the ambition to reach *moksha* will not be there. When you feel that even the desire to reach moksha has disappeared, you have reached moksha. Now you are free, because desire is the bondage. Even the desire for liberation is a bondage. Even the desire to be desireless is a bondage.

Whenever the desire for anything disappears, you move into the unknown. The meditation has reached its end. Then *sansar* is moksha: this very world is liberation. Then this shore is the other shore.

27

The Warrior

Being a businessman and a professional, how can I be a warrior at the same time? Am I going to miss enlightenment?

TO BE A warrior doesn't mean to be a soldier, it is a quality of the mind. You can be a businessman and be a warrior; you can be a warrior and a businessman.

'Businessman' means a quality of the mind which is always bargaining, trying to give less and get more. That's what I mean when I say 'businessman': trying to give less and get more, always bargaining, always thinking about profit. A warrior is again a quality of the mind, the quality of the gambler, not of the bargainer, the quality which can stake everything this way or that—a non-compromising mind.

If a businessman thinks of enlightenment, he thinks of it as a commodity like many other commodities. He has a list: he has to make a big palace, he has to purchase this and that, and, in the end, he has to purchase enlightenment also. But enlightenment is always the last: when everything is done, then; when nothing remains to be done, then. And that enlightenment is also to be purchased because he understands only money.

It happened that a great and rich man came to Mahavira. He was really very rich; he could purchase anything, even kingdoms. Even kings borrowed money from him.

He came to Mahavira and said, 'I have been hearing so much about meditation, and during the time you have been here, you have created a craze in people; everybody is talking about meditation. What *is* meditation? How much does it cost and can I purchase it?'

Mahavira hesitated, so the man said, 'Don't you think about the cost at all. You simply say and I will pay; there is no problem about it.'

How to talk to this man?—Mahavira was at a loss as to what to say to him. Finally, Mahavira said, 'Go . . . . In your town, there is a man, a very poor man; he may be willing to sell his meditation. He has achieved it, and he is so poor that he may be ready to sell it.'

The man thanked Mahavira, rushed to the poor man, knocked on his door and said, 'How much do you want for your meditation? I want to purchase your meditation.'

The man started laughing. He said, 'You can purchase *me*, that's okay. But how can I give you my meditation? It is a quality of my being, it is not a commodity.'

But businessmen have always been thinking in this way. They donate to purchase something, they create temples to purchase something. They give, but their giving is never a giving; it is always to get something, it is an investment.

When I say to you to be a warrior, I mean to be a gambler, to put everything at stake. Then enlightenment becomes a question of life and death, not a commodity, and you are ready to throw away everything for it. And you are not thinking about the profit.

People come to me and ask, 'What will we gain out of meditation? What is the purpose of it? What will be the profit out of it? If one hour is devoted to meditation, what will be the gain?' Their whole life is economy.

A warrior is not after gain; a warrior is after a peak, after a peak of experiencing. What does a warrior gain when he fights in a war? Your soldiers are not warriors any longer, they are just servants. Warriors are no longer on this earth because the whole thing is being done by technology. You drop a bomb on Hiroshima; the dropper is not a warrior. Any child can do that, any madman can do that—really, only a madman can do it. Dropping a bomb on Hiroshima is not being a fighter or a warrior.

War is no longer the same as it was in the past; now anybody can do it, and sooner or later only mechanical devices will do it. A plane without a pilot can do it—and the plane is not a warrior. The quality is lost.

The warrior was facing, encountering the enemy, face to face. Just imagine two people with drawn swords encountering each other: can they think? If they think, they will miss. Thinking stops; when swords are drawn, thinking stops. They cannot plan because if they plan, in that moment, the other will hit. They move spontaneously, they become no-minds. The danger is so much, the possibility of death is so near, that the mind cannot be allowed to function. The mind needs time; in emergencies, the mind cannot be allowed. When you are sitting on your chair, you can think, but when you are facing an enemy, you cannot think.

If you pass through a street, a dark street, and suddenly see a snake, a dangerous snake sitting there, what will you do? Will you start thinking? No, you will jump. And this jump will not be out of your mind because the mind needs time, and snakes don't have any time; they don't have any mind. The snake will strike you—so the mind cannot be allowed. While facing a snake, you jump, and that jump comes out of your being; it comes before thought. You jump first and then you think.

This is what I mean by the quality of a warrior: action comes without thinking, action is without mind; action is total. You can become a warrior without going to war, there is no need to go to war.

The whole of life is an emergency, and everywhere there are enemies, snakes, and ferocious wild animals ready to attack you. The whole of life is a war. If you are alert, you will see that the whole of life is a war, and any moment you can die; so the emergency is permanent. Be alert, be like a warrior as if moving amidst the enemy. Any moment, from anywhere, death can jump on you; don't allow the mind. And be a gambler—only gamblers can take this jump. The jump is so much that those who think of profit cannot take it. It is a risk, the greatest risk; you may be lost and nothing may be gained. When you come to me, you may lose everything and you may not gain anything.

I will repeat one of Jesus's sayings: 'Whosoever clings to life, whosoever tries to preserve it, will lose it; and whosoever is ready to lose it, will preserve it.' This is talking in the language of a gambler: Lose it—this is the way to preserve it. Die—that is the way to reach eternal life, the immortal life.

When I say a businessman, I say a calculating, cunning mind. Don't be cunning minds. No child is ever a businessman, and it is difficult to find an old man who is not a businessman. Every child is a warrior and every old man is a businessman. How every warrior becomes a businessman is a long story: the whole society, education, culture, conditioning, makes you more and more fearful, afraid. You cannot take a risk, and everything that is beautiful *is* risky.

Love is a risk. Life is a risk. God is a risk. God is the greatest risk, and through mathematics, you will not reach; only through taking the ultimate risk, putting everything that you have at stake. And you don't know the unknown; the known you risk, and the unknown you don't know.

The business mind will say, 'What are you doing— losing that which you have for that which no one knows exists or not? Preserve that which is in hand and don't long for the unknown.' The warrior mind says, 'The known has been known already, now there is nothing in it; it has become a burden and to carry it is useless. The unknown must be known now, and I must risk the known for the unknown.'

And if you can risk, totally risk, not preserving anything, not playing tricks with yourself, not withholding anything, suddenly, the unknown envelops you. And when it comes, you become aware that it is not only the unknown, it is the unknowable. It is not against the known, it is beyond the known. To move in that darkness, to move in that uncharted place without any maps and without any pathways, to move alone into that absolute, the quality of the warrior is needed.

Many of you still have a little of it left because you were once children; you were all warriors, you were all dreamers of the unknown. That childhood is hidden but it cannot be destroyed; it is there, it still has its own corner in your being. Allow it to function; be childlike and you will be warriors again. That's what I mean.

And don't feel depressed because you run a shop and you are a businessman. Don't feel depressed; you can be a warrior anywhere. To take risks is a quality of the mind, a childlike quality—to trust and to move beyond that which is secure.

The greatest warrior has nothing to do with war. He has nothing to do with fighting others. He has something to do inside himself. And it is not a fight, although it brings victory; it is not a war, not a conflict. But one has to be a warrior because one has to be very alert just like a warrior.

One has to be very watchful, very meditative, because if one is moving in the darkest continent in existence . . . Ultimately, there is light, infinite light, but first one has to pass through a great dark night of the soul. There are all kinds of pitfalls, all possibilities of going astray and there are all kinds of inner enemies. They have not to be killed or destroyed; they have to be transformed, they have to be converted into friends. Anger has to be transformed into compassion, lust has to be transformed into love, and so on and so forth. So it is not a war, but certainly one needs to be a warrior.

That's how, in Japan, the whole world of the samurai, the warrior, came out of meditation and all kinds of martial arts became paths towards inner peace. Swordsmanship became one of the most meditative things in Japan. One has to be very alert because a single moment of unconsciousness, and you are finished.

The real swordsman becomes so alert that before the other person attacks him, he knows. Before the thought of attack has even crossed the other's mind, he has prepared himself. He is ready. His watchfulness becomes so deep that he starts reading the thoughts of the other. It is said that if two real samurais fight, nobody can win. The fight can continue but nobody can win because both will be reading the other's mind. And before you can attack, the other is already there to defend.

Swordsmanship became one of the greatest sources of enlightenment. It seems strange, but Japan has done many really strange things. From tea drinking to swordsmanship, everything has been changed into meditation. In fact, the whole of life can be transformed into meditation, because meditation simply means becoming more aware.

So go inwards and be more aware. One day victory is yours—that is absolutely certain. You just have to fulfil the requirement: you have to be totally aware.

It happened once, a Zen samurai, a Zen warrior, had come home early from the front, and he found the servant making love to his wife. Being a man of Zen, he said to the servant, 'Don't be worried, just finish your job. I am waiting outside. You will have to take a sword in your hand and fight with me. It is perfectly okay whatever is happening. I am waiting outside.'

This poor servant started trembling. He does not even know how to hold a sword, and his master is a famous warrior; he will chop off his head in a single blow. So he ran out from the back door to the Zen master who was also the master of the warrior. He said to the master, 'I have got into trouble. It is all my fault, but it has happened.'

The master listened to his story and said, 'There is no need to be worried. I will teach you how to hold the sword, and I will also tell you that it does not matter that your master is a great warrior. All that matters is spontaneity. And in spontaneity, you will be better, because he seems to be confident: there is no question of this servant surviving. It will be almost like a cat playing with a rat. So don't be worried. Be total, and hit him hard, because this is your only chance of living, survival. So don't be half-hearted, don't be conditional, thinking that perhaps he may forgive you. He will never forgive you—

you will have to fight with him. You have provoked and challenged him. But there is no problem: as far as I can see, you will end up as the winner.'

The servant could not believe it, and the master said, 'You should understand that I am his master also, and I know that he will behave according to his training. Knowing perfectly well that he is going to win, he cannot be unconditional—and you have no other alternative than to be unconditional. Just be total. You don't know which place to hit, how to hit, so hit anywhere. Just go crazy!'

The servant said, 'If you say so, I will do it. In fact, there is no chance of my survival, so why not do it totally!'

Seeing that the time had come, he learned how to hold the sword, and he came back and challenged his master, 'Now come on!'

The samurai could not believe it. He was thinking the servant would fall at his feet and cry and weep and say, 'Just forgive me!' But instead of that, the servant roared like a lion, and he had got a sword from the Zen master! He recognized the sword, and asked, 'From where did you get it?'

The servant said, 'From your master. Now come, let it be decided once and for all. Either I will survive or you will survive, but both cannot.' The samurai felt a little tremble in his heart, but still he thought, 'How can he manage? It is years' training . . . . I have been fighting for years in wars, and this poor servant . . . .' But he had to take out his sword.

The servant went really crazy. Not knowing where to hit, he was hitting here and there and just . . . The samurai was at a loss, because he could fight with any warrior who knew how to fight—but this man knows nothing and he is doing all kinds of things! The servant pushed him to the wall, and the samurai had to ask him, 'Please forgive me.

You will kill me. You don't know how to fight—what are you doing?'

The servant said, 'It is not a question of doing. It is my last moment; I will do everything with totality.'

The servant became the winner, and the warrior went to the master and asked, 'What miracle have you done? Within five minutes, he became such a great warrior, and he was making such blows, so stupid that he could have killed me. He knows nothing but he could have killed me. He pushed me to the wall of my house, his sword on my chest. I had to ask to be forgiven and tell him that whatever he is doing, it is perfectly okay and to continue.'

The master said, 'You have to learn a lesson, that it is finally the totality, the unconditional absoluteness . . . whether it brings defeat or victory does not matter. What matters is that the man was total, and the total man never is defeated. His totality is his victory.'

28

The Gambler

What does it mean to live dangerously?

TO LIVE DANGEROUSLY means to live. If you don't live
dangerously, you don't live. Living flowers only in danger.
Living never flowers in security; it flowers only in insecurity.

If you start getting secure, you become a stagnant
pool. Then your energy is no longer moving. Then you are
afraid, because one never knows how to go into the
unknown. And why take the risk?—the known is more
secure. Then you get obsessed with the familiar. You go on
getting fed up with it, you are bored with it, you feel
miserable in it, but still it seems familiar and comfortable.
At least it is known. The unknown creates a trembling in
you. The very idea of the unknown and you start feeling
unsafe.

There are only two types of people in the world.
People who want to live comfortably . . . . They are
seeking death; they want a comfortable grave. And people
who want to *live*. They choose to live dangerously, because
life thrives only when there is risk. Have you ever gone
climbing the mountains? The higher the climb, the fresher
you feel, the younger you feel. The greater the danger of

falling, the bigger the abyss by the side, the more alive you are . . . between life and death, when you are just hanging between life and death. Then there is no boredom, then there is no dust of the past, no desire for the future. Then the present moment is very sharp, like a flame. It is enough. You live in the here and now . . . Or surfing or skiing or gliding: wherever there is a risk of losing life, there is tremendous joy because the risk of losing life makes you tremendously alive. Hence, people are attracted to dangerous sports.

People go climbing mountains. Somebody asked Hillary, 'Why did you try to climb Everest? Why?' And he said, 'Because it is there—a constant challenge.' It was risky, many people had died before. For almost sixty, seventy years, groups had been going, and it was almost a certain death. But still people were going. What was the attraction?

Reaching higher, going farther away from the settled, the routine life, you again become wild, you again become part of the animal world. You again live like a tiger or a lion or like a river. You again soar like a bird into the skies, farther and farther away. And each moment the security, bank balance, wife, husband, family, society, church, respectability—all are fading further and further away, becoming more and more distant. You become alone.

This is why people are so interested in sports. But that too is not real danger because you can become very skilled. You can learn it, you can be trained for it. It is a very calculated risk—if you allow me the expression, a calculated risk. You can train for mountaineering and you can take all precautions. Or driving, speed-driving. You can go a hundred miles per hour. It is dangerous, it is thrilling. But you can become really skilful at it, and the danger is only for outsiders; for you, it is not. And even if it is there, it is very marginal. And then, these risks are only physical risks, only the body is involved.

When I say to you, live dangerously, I mean not only take bodily risks, but psychological risks, and finally spiritual risks. Religion is a spiritual risk. It is going to such heights from where maybe there is no return.

When I say live dangerously, I mean don't live the life of ordinary respectability—you are mayor in a town, or member of the cooperation. This is not life. Or you are a minister, or you have a good profession and are earning well and money goes on accumulating in the bank and everything is going perfectly well. When everything is going perfectly well, simply see it—you are dying and nothing is happening. People may respect you, and when you die, a great procession will follow you. Good, that's all. And in newspapers, your pictures will be published and there will be editorials, and then people will forget about you. And you lived your whole life only for these things.

Watch—one can miss one's whole life for ordinary, mundane things. To be spiritual means to understand that these small things should not be given too much importance. I am not saying that they are meaningless. I am saying that they are meaningful, but not as meaningful as you think.

Money is needed. It is a need. But money is not the goal and cannot be the goal. A house is needed, certainly. It is a need. I am not an ascetic and I don't want you to destroy your houses and escape to the Himalayas. The house is needed—but the house is needed for *you*. Don't misunderstand it. As I see people, the whole thing has gone topsy-turvy. They exist as if they are needed for the house. They go on working for the house. As if they are needed for the bank balance—they simply go on collecting money and then they die. And they had never lived. They never had a single moment of throbbing, streaming life. They were just imprisoned in security, familiarity, respectability.

Then if you feel bored, it is natural. People come to me and they say they feel very bored. They feel fed up, stuck. What to do? They think that just by repeating a *mantra*, they will again become alive. It is not so easy. They will have to change their whole life pattern.

Love, but don't think that tomorrow the woman will be available to you. Don't expect that. Don't reduce the woman to a wife. Then you are living dangerously. Don't reduce the man to a husband, because a husband is an ugly thing. Let your man be your man and your woman your woman. And don't make your tomorrow predictable. Expect nothing and be ready for everything. That's what I mean when I say live dangerously.

What do we do? We fall in love with a woman and immediately we start going to the court, or to the registry office, or to the church to get married. I'm not saying don't get married. It is a formality. Good, satisfy the society. But deep in your mind never possess the woman. Never for a single moment say, 'You belong to me'—because how can a person belong to you? And when you start possessing the woman, she will start possessing you. Then you both are no longer in love. You are just crushing and killing each other, paralysing each other.

Love—but don't degrade your love through marriage. Work—work is needed—but don't let work become your only life.

Play should remain your life, your centre of life. Work should be a means towards play. Work in the office and work in the factory and work in the shop, but just to have time, opportunity, to play. Don't let your life be reduced to just a working routine—because the goal of life is *play*.

Play means doing something for its own sake.

You come to me even to meditate, and you take

meditation as work. You think something has to be done to achieve God. It is nonsense. Meditation cannot be that way. You have to play, you have to take it as fun. You do not have to be serious about it. You have to enjoy. When you enjoy it, it develops. When you start taking it as work, as a duty to be done—because you have to do, you have to achieve *moksha*, *nirvana*, liberation—then you have brought your foolish categories into the world of play.

Meditation is play, it is *leela*. You enjoy it for its own sake.

If you enjoy many more things for their own sake, you will be more alive. Of course, your life will always be at risk, danger. But that's how life has to be. Risk is part of it. In fact, the better part of it is risk, the best part of it is risk. The most beautiful part of it is risk. It is every moment a risk. You may not be aware. You breathe in, you breathe out. There is risk. Even breathing out, who knows whether the breath will come back or not? It is not certain, there is no guarantee.

But there are a few people whose whole religion is security. Even if they talk about God, they talk about God as the supreme security. If they think about God, they think only because they are afraid. If they go to pray and meditate, they are going just in order that they remain in the good books—in God's good books. 'If there is a God, he will know that I was a regular church-goer, a regular worshipper. I can claim that.' Even their prayer is just a means.

To live dangerously means to live life as if each moment is its own end. Each moment has its own intrinsic value. And you are not afraid. You know death is there and you accept the fact that death is there, and you are not hiding against death. In fact, you go and encounter death. You enjoy those moments of encountering death—

physically, psychologically, spiritually.

Enjoying those moments where you come directly in contact with death, where death becomes almost a reality, is what I mean when I say live dangerously.

Love brings you face to face with death. Meditation brings you face to face with death. Coming to a master is coming to your own death. Facing somebody who has disappeared is entering an abyss in which you can be lost, and you can become one who never returns.

Those who are courageous, they go headlong. They search all opportunities of danger. Their life philosophy is not that of insurance companies but that of a mountain climber, a glider, a surfer. And not only in the outside seas do they surf, they surf in their innermost seas. And not only on the outside do they climb Alps and Himalayas, they seek inner peaks.

But remember one thing—never forget the art of risking, never, never. Always remain capable of risking. And wherever you can find an opportunity to risk, never miss it, and you will never be a loser. Risk is the only guarantee for being truly alive.

29

The Creator

In the past, all famous artists have been well-known for their bohemian style of life. Please can you say something about creativity and discipline?

THE BOHEMIAN LIFE is the only life worth living! All other kinds of lives are only lukewarm; they are more ways of committing slow suicide than ways of living life passionately and intensely. In the past, it was inevitable that the artist had to live in rebellion, because creativity is the greatest rebellion in existence. If you want to create, you have to get rid of all conditionings; otherwise, your creativity will be nothing but copying, it will be just a carbon copy. You can be creative only if you are an individual, you cannot create as a part of the mob psychology. The mob psychology is uncreative; it lives a life that is more a drag. It knows no dance, no song, no joy; it is mechanical.

Of course, there are a few things you will get from society only if you are mechanical. Respectability you will get, honours you will get. Universities will confer D. Litts on you, countries will give you gold medals, you may finally become a Nobel laureate. But this whole thing is ugly.

A real man of genius will discard all this nonsense, because this is bribery. Giving the Nobel prize to a person simply means that your services to the establishment are respected, that you are honoured because you have been a good slave, obedient, that you have not gone astray, that you have followed the well-trodden path.

The creator cannot follow the well-trodden path. He has to search and find out his own way. He has to inquire in the jungles of life, he has to go alone, he has to be a dropout from the mob mind, from the collective psychology. The collective mind is the lowest mind in the world; even the so-called idiots are a little more superior than the collective idiocy. But collectivity has its own bribes: it respects people, honours people, if they go on insisting that the way of the collective mind is the only right way.

It was out of sheer necessity that in the past, creators of all kinds—the painters, the dancers, the musicians, the poets, the sculptors—had to renounce respectability. They had to live a kind of bohemian life, the life of a vagabond; that was the only possibility for them to be creative. This need not be so in the future. If you understand me, if you feel what I am saying has truth in it, in future everybody should live individually and there will be no need for a bohemian life. The bohemian life is the by-product of a fixed, orthodox, conventional, respectable life.

My effort is to destroy the collective mind and to make each individual free to be himself or herself. Then there is no problem; then you can live as you want to live. In fact, humanity will really only be born the day the individual is respected in his rebellion. Humanity has still not been born; it is still in the womb. What you see as humanity is only a very hocus-pocus phenomenon. Unless we give individual freedom to each person, absolute freedom to each person to be himself, to exist in his own way . . . .

And, of course, he has not to interfere with anybody—that is part of freedom. Nobody should interfere with anybody.

But in the past everybody has been poking his nose into everybody else's affairs—even into things which are absolutely private, which have nothing to do with society. For example, you fall in love with a woman—what has that got to do with society? It is purely a personal phenomenon, it is not of the marketplace. If two people are agreeing to commune in love, society should not come into it. But the society comes into it with all its paraphernalia, in direct ways, in indirect ways. The policeman will stand between the lovers; the magistrate will stand between the lovers; and, if that is not enough, then societies have created a super-policeman, God, who will take care of you.

The idea of God is that of a peeping Tom who does not even allow you privacy in your bathroom, who goes on looking through the keyhole, watching what you are doing. This is ugly. All the religions of the world say God continuously watches you—this is ugly. What kind of God is this? Has he got no other business but to watch everybody, follow everybody? Seems to be the supreme-most detective!

Humanity needs a new soil—the soil of freedom. Bohemianism was a reaction, a necessary reaction, but if my vision succeeds, there will be no bohemianism because there will be no so-called collective mind trying to dominate people. Then everybody will be at ease with himself. Of course, you have not to interfere with anybody, but as far as your life is concerned, you have to live it on your own terms. Then only is there creativity. Creativity is the fragrance of individual freedom.

You ask me: '*Please can you say something about creativity and discipline?*'

Discipline is a beautiful word, but it has been misused as all other beautiful words have been misused in the past. The word discipline comes from the same root as the word *disciple*; the root meaning of the word is *a process of learning*. One who is ready to learn is a disciple, and the process of being ready to learn is discipline.

The knowledgeable person is never ready to learn because he already thinks he knows; he is very centred in his so-called knowledge. His knowledge is nothing but a nourishment for his ego. He cannot be a disciple, he cannot be in true discipline.

Socrates says: 'I know only one thing, that I know nothing.' That is the beginning of discipline. When you don't know anything, of course, a great longing to inquire, explore, investigate arises. And the moment you start learning, another factor follows inevitably: whatsoever you have learned has to be dropped continuously, otherwise it will become knowledge and knowledge will prevent further learning.

The real man of discipline never accumulates; each moment he dies to whatsoever he has come to know and again becomes ignorant. That ignorance is really luminous. It is one of the most beautiful experiences in existence to be in a state of luminous not-knowing. When you are in that state of not-knowing, you are open. There is no barrier, you are ready to explore. The Hindus cannot do it; they are already knowledgeable. The Mohammedans cannot do it, the Christians cannot do it.

Discipline has been misinterpreted. People have been telling others to discipline their life, to do this, not to do that. Thousands of shoulds and should-nots have been imposed on man, and when a man lives with thousands of shoulds and should-nots, he cannot be creative. He is a prisoner; everywhere he will come across a wall.

The creative person has to dissolve all shoulds and should-nots. He needs freedom and space, vast space, he needs the whole sky and all the stars, only then can his innermost spontaneity start growing.

So remember, my meaning of discipline is not that of any Ten Commandments; I am not giving you any discipline; I am simply giving you an insight into how to keep on learning and never become knowledgeable. Your discipline has to come from your very heart, it has to be *yours*—and there is a great difference. When somebody else gives you the discipline, it can never fit you; it will be like wearing somebody else's clothes. Either they will be too loose or too tight, and you will always feel a little bit silly in them.

Mohammed has given a discipline to the Mohammedans; it may have been good for him, but it cannot be good for anybody else. Buddha has given a discipline to millions of Buddhists; it may have been good for him, but it cannot be good for anybody else. A discipline is an individual phenomenon; whenever you borrow it, you start living according to set principles, dead principles. And life is never dead; life is constantly changing each moment. Life is a flux.

Heraclitus is right: you cannot step in the same river twice. In fact, I would like to say you cannot step in the same river even once, the river is so fast moving! One has to be alert to, watchful of, each situation and its nuances, and one has to respond to the situation according to the moment, not according to any ready-made answers given by others.

Do you see the stupidity of humanity? Five thousand years ago Manu gave a discipline to the Hindus and they are still following it. Three thousand years ago Moses gave a discipline to the Jews and they are still following it. Five thousand years ago Adinatha gave his discipline to the

Jainas and they are still following it. The whole world is being driven crazy by these disciplines! They are out of date, they should have been buried long ago. You are carrying corpses and those corpses are stinking. And when you live surrounded by corpses, what kind of a life can you have?

I teach you the moment and the freedom of the moment and the responsibility of the moment. One thing may be right this moment and may become wrong the next moment. Don't try to be consistent, otherwise you will be dead. Only dead people are consistent.

Try to be alive, with all its inconsistencies, and live each moment without any reference to the past, without any reference to the future either. Live the moment in the context of the moment, and your response will be total. And that totality has beauty and that totality is creativity. Then whatsoever you do will have a beauty of its own.

30

Ageing

Will you say something to me about old age?

A PERSON CAN either grow old or grow up. The person who only grows old has not lived at all. He has passed time, but he has not lived. All his life is nothing but repression. I teach you not to grow old. That does not mean you will not become old, it means I give you another dimension: growing up. Certainly, you will grow old but that will only be as far as the body is concerned. But your consciousness, you, will not grow old; you will only grow up. You will go on growing in maturity.

But all the religions of the world have been committing such crimes that they cannot be forgiven. They have not been teaching you how to live, they have been teaching you how *not* to live—how to renounce life, how to renounce the world. This world, according to the various religions, is a punishment. You are in jail. So the only thing is to try to escape from the jail as quickly as possible. This is not true.

Life is not a punishment. Life is so valuable that it cannot be a punishment, it is a reward. And you should be thankful to existence that it has chosen you—to breathe through you, to love through you, to sing through you, to dance through you.

If one keeps growing up in maturity and understanding, one never becomes old; one is always young because one is always learning. Learning keeps you young. One is always young because one is not burdened with repressions. And because one is weightless, one feels as if one is just a child—a newcomer to this beautiful earth.

I have heard that three priests were going to Pittsburgh. They reached the window to purchase their tickets and the woman at the window who was selling the tickets was extraordinarily beautiful. Her clothes were almost negligible—she had beautiful breasts—and with a V-cut.

The youngest of the priests went up to the window, but he had forgotten all about the journey: he was only seeing those beautiful breasts. The woman asked, 'What can I do for you?'

He said, 'Three tickets for Titsburgh.'

The woman freaked out. She said, 'You are a priest!'

The second one came up and pushed him aside. He told the woman, 'Don't get angry, he's just new, immature. You just give us three tickets for Titsburgh.'

The woman looked at him: were all these men mad or something?

'... And remember one thing: I would like to have the change in nipples and dimes.'

Now the woman started shouting and screaming, 'This is too much!'

The oldest priest came over and said, 'My daughter, don't be angry. These fellows stay in the monastery, they do not come out, they don't see anything. You should have a little understanding about their life: they have renounced life. Just calm down. Now, we need three tickets for Titsburgh.'

The woman could not believe them—all three seemed to be idiots!

The old priest said, 'Remember one thing, I admonish you: use better clothes to cover your beautiful body. Otherwise, remember, on judgement day, Saint Finger will point his Peter at you!'

This is the situation of the obsessed person. The more you deny life, the more you become obsessed with the same life. Up to now, we have not allowed man to live a nonobsessional life.

All religions and governments are angry with me for the simple reason that I am in favour of you, your freedom and a nonobsessional life—a pure, natural flow, joyous, making the whole of life a paradise.

We are not searching for any paradise in the clouds. If it is there, we will get hold of it, but first we have to make a paradise here on earth; that will be our preparation. If we can live in a paradise on earth, wherever paradise is, it is ours; nobody else can claim it—at least not these priests and monks and nuns! All these people are bound towards hell, because on the surface, they are one thing, and inside it is just the opposite. Try to be natural.

Risk everything to be natural and you will not be at a loss.

✱

Why is there such an expression as 'dirty old man'?
I am getting old and I suspect people are beginning
to think about me in exactly those words.

It is because of a repressive society since long that the dirty old man exists. It is because of your saints, your priests, your puritans, that the dirty old man exists.

If people are allowed to live their sexual life joyously, by the time they are nearing forty-two—remember, I am saying forty-two, not eighty-four—just when they are nearing forty-two, sex will start losing its grip on them. Just as sex arises and becomes very powerful by the time one is fourteen, in exactly the same way, by the time one is forty-two, it starts disappearing. It is a natural course. And when sex disappears, the old man has love, has compassion, of a totally different kind. There is no lust in his love, no desire, he wants to get nothing out of it. His love has a purity, an innocence; his love is a joy.

Sex gives you pleasure. And sex gives you pleasure only when you have gone into sex; then pleasure is the end result. If sex has become irrelevant—not repressed, but because you experienced it so deeply that it is no longer of any value . . . . You have known it, and knowledge always brings freedom. You have known it totally, and because you have known it, the mystery is finished, there is nothing more to explore. In that knowing, the whole energy, the sexual energy, is transmuted into love, compassion. Then one gives out of joy. Then the old man is the most beautiful man in the world, the cleanest man in the world.

There is no such expression in any language as the 'clean old man.' I have never heard it. But this expression, the 'dirty old man,' exists in almost all languages. The reason is that the body becomes old, the body becomes tired, the body wants to get rid of all sexuality—but the mind, because of repressed desires, still hankers. When the body is not capable, and the mind continuously haunts you for something which the body is incapable of doing, the old man is in a mess. His eyes are sexual, lusty; his body dead and dull. And his mind goes on goading him. He starts having a dirty look, a dirty face; he starts having something ugly in him.

It reminds me of the story of the man who overheard his wife and her sister discussing his frequent out-of-town business trips. The sister kept suggesting that the wife should worry about her husband being unchaperoned at those posh resort convention hotels with so many attractive, unattached career women around.

'Me worry?' said the wife. 'Why, he'd never cheat on me. He's too loyal, too decent . . . too old.'

The body sooner or later becomes old—it is bound to become old—but if you have not lived your desires, they will clamour around you, they are bound to create something ugly in you. Either the old man becomes the most beautiful man in the world, because he attains to an innocence the same as that of a child, or even far deeper than the innocence of a child—he becomes a sage. But if desires are still there, running like an undercurrent, he is caught in a turmoil.

A very old man was arrested while attempting to sexually molest a young woman. Seeing such an old man, eighty-four, in court, the magistrate reduced the charge from rape to assault with a dead weapon.

If you are becoming old, remember that old age is the climax of life. Remember that old age can be the most beautiful experience—because the child has hopes for the future, he lives in the future. He has great desires to do this, to do that. Every child thinks that he is going to be somebody special—Alexander the Great, Josef Stalin, Mao Zedong. He lives in desires and in the future. The young man is too possessed by the instincts, all the instincts, exploding in him. Sex is there: the young man is possessed by such great natural forces that he cannot be free. Ambition is there, and time is running out fast, and he has to do something and he has to be something. All those hopes and desires and fantasies of childhood have to be fulfilled; he is in a great rush, in a hurry.

The old man knows that those childish desires were really childish. He knows that all those days of youth and turmoil are gone. He is in the same state as when the storm has gone and silence prevails. That silence can be of tremendous beauty, depth, richness. If the old man is really mature, which is very rarely the case, he will be beautiful. But people only grow in age, they don't grow up. Hence the problem.

Grow up, become more mature, become more alert and aware. And old age is the last opportunity given to you: before death comes, prepare. And how does one prepare for death? By becoming more meditative.

If some lurking desires are still there, and the body is getting old and it is not capable of fulfilling those desires, don't be worried. Meditate over those desires, watch, be aware. Just by being aware and watchful and alert, those desires and the energy contained in them can be transmuted. But before death comes, be free of all desires.

When I say be free of all desires, I simply mean be free of all objects of desires. Then there is pure longing. That pure longing is divine, that pure longing is God. Then there is pure creativity with no object, with no address, with no direction, with no destination—just pure energy, a pool of energy, going nowhere. That's what buddhahood is.

31

The Master

*To the Western world, the terms 'freedom' and
'the master' are virtually mutually exclusive. For
those who have met you, this is wildly inaccurate.
How do you redefine freedom and the master for
Western understanding?*

THE WESTERN WORLD has not come in contact with the
tremendous reality that happens in the meeting of a master
and a disciple. Of course, it is not visible. It is just like
love, but far greater and far deeper and far more mysterious.

The West has known saints and followers. The saints
demand surrender, the saints demand faith. And the moment
you become faithful, you are no more; your whole
individuality has been erased. Then you are a Christian
and you are a Jew, but you are not you. The phenomenon
of the master and the disciple happened in the East in its
golden days, when there were people like Lao Tzu and
Zarathustra and Gautam Buddha. They created a totally
new kind of relationship.

Everybody cannot paint like a Picasso, nor can
everybody be a Michelangelo. The West has missed having
a Gautam Buddha. Jesus is not at all a comparison to him.

Jesus is simply a Jew, believing in all the Jewish dogmas. He is faithful—in fact, a little too much. Gautam Buddha is a rebel; he is not a follower of anyone. Nor is Lao Tzu a follower of anyone. They don't have any scriptures, they don't have any belief systems. They have searched on their own, alone—risking, because they are moving away from the crowd on the lonely path, not knowing where this journey is going to end, but trusting their heart, experiencing small indications that peace is growing, that love is flowering, that a new fragrance has come to their being, that their eyes are no longer full of dust, of the past. A tremendous clarity and transparency . . . and they know they are on the right path.

There is no guide, and you will not meet anybody on the path to inquire how far the destination is. It is a flight from the alone to the alone. But once a man finds truth on his own, naturally he becomes aware that no organized religion is needed—it is a hindrance—that no priest, no mediators are needed; they will not allow you to reach the truth. Such a man, who has found the truth, becomes a master.

The difference is subtle and has to be understood. The disciple is not a follower; the disciple has simply fallen in love. You don't call lovers followers. Something has clicked in his being, in the presence of someone. It is not a question of him being convinced about his ideas. It is not a conviction, it is not a conversion, it is a transformation. The moment a seeker comes in contact with one who has found, a great synchronicity happens. Looking into each others' eyes, without saying a word, something that they have never dreamt of suddenly becomes the greatest reality.

It is not belief, because belief is always in philosophies, in ideologies. It is not faith, because faith is in fictions for which nobody can find an argument or evidence—it is trust. What relates the master to the disciple is trust. Trust is the highest flowering of love. And how can love make anyone a slave? The very fact that it is love that joins the master and the disciple is enough indication that he will prepare every possibility for the disciple's freedom; otherwise, he will be betraying love and no master can betray love.

Love is the ultimate reality. He has to fulfil it in his actions, in his words, in his relations, in his silences. Whatever he does, he has to fulfil only one thing: that is his love. And if a person is groping in the dark, a disciple has come to him . . . only a priest can exploit him, a politician can exploit him. They are in search of followers— both the priest and the politician. The politician and the priest are agreed on one point, that they need followers; only then can they become somebody. And they have divided their territories: the politician has taken the mundane world and the priest the spiritual. Between the two of them, they have made the whole of humanity slaves. They have destroyed everybody's freedom.

The greatest contribution has come from a few masters who attained not only their own freedom but also the freedom of those who loved them. It is simply inconceivable: if you love me, how can I enslave you? If you love me, I will only rejoice in your freedom. When I see you opening your wings into the sky towards the unknown, the far away, the mysterious, that will be my joy; not that you are tethered to a certain dogma, creed, cult, religion, philosophy. These are all different names of chains, manufactured by different kinds of people, but their purpose is the same.

Because the West has not known masters . . . . It has known popes, it has known prophets, it has known saviours, it has known saints. It is absolutely unaware that there is a dimension it has missed, and that dimension is the most valuable dimension . . . . Because it has missed it, a great misunderstanding has arisen. It happens . . . you know the beautiful parable of Aesop.

A fox is trying, jumping as hard as possible, to reach the beautiful, ripe grapes hanging just above his head. But his jump is smaller than the height of the grapes. Tired, perspiring, having fallen many times, he looks around to see if anybody is watching.

A small rabbit, just hiding in a small bush, was watching. This was dangerous, this rabbit would spread the news all over. The fox walked away from the grapes. The rabbit followed and asked, 'Uncle, just one question. What happened? Why could you not reach the grapes?'

The fox was very angry. He said, 'I suspected, the moment I saw you, that you were going to spread rumours about me. I have not chosen to take those grapes because they are not ripe. And if I hear anybody talking about those grapes, I will kill you, because you are the only witness.'

It is a small parable, but it contains immense meaning: that which you cannot reach, you start condemning—the grapes are not ripe.

You are asking, 'To the Western world, the terms "freedom" and "the master" are virtually mutually exclusive; for those who have met you this is wildly inaccurate. How do you redefine "freedom" and "the master" for the Western understanding?'

The word master creates confusion. It gives you the idea that you have become a slave, somebody has become your master. In the East, the word is used in the sense that you have become master of yourself, that you are no longer a slave, that you have attained freedom. Different languages, developed in different climates by different people, different experiences, are bound to create such kinds of confusion.

To be master of oneself has never been a goal in the Western consciousness—it has always been how to conquer others, how to be a master of *others*. It is difficult to translate many Eastern words into Western language. The same difficulty is there if you want to translate quantum physics into Eastern languages; you will not find the right words, because before language comes in, the experience has to be there. Experience creates language. And if you try, very funny things are bound to happen. The eastern word for master is *acharya*. The word acharya means one who lives his life authentically, according to his own consciousness and awareness. And if you come close to such a person, what can he give you? Being with him, you will learn only one thing: how to live in freedom, awareness, in deep integrity and dignity. We are using the word master for acharya.

The word disciple is more fortunate, because the eastern word shishya and the word disciple have exactly the same meanings—for different reasons, but the meanings are the same. The disciple is one who is trying to learn something. The root meaning of the word disciple is the same as the root meaning of the word discipline. It means, preparing yourself to learn, to understand. It is perfectly good as it is; it can be used.

As far as the word master is concerned . . . . The disciple has just fallen in love with the man and wants to learn the same freedom, the same sincerity, the same integrity and height of consciousness. The question of surrender does not arise, and the question of belief does not arise. In the presence of the master, in the climate of the master, disciples start growing into new dimensions, which they did not know they were carrying within themselves as potentials. The master does not give them anything except his love—that too it cannot be said he gives. It is simply showering, just the way the sun showers its rays on flowers, birds, animals; whoever comes close to the master is showered with love.

If you are searching, if you are ready to learn, if you are not already learned, if you are not already prejudiced, if you are not already faithful, if you have not sold your soul already to some theology, to some religion, to some ideology, just being close to the master, something starts transpiring. It is a transmission of the lamp. That's how it has been known in the East: a transmission of light from one heart, which has come to its own fire, to another heart which is groping in darkness. Just coming closer . . . Think of two candles, one lit and one unlit, coming closer and closer. A moment comes when you will be suddenly amazed—both candles are lit. The flame has jumped to the other candle. Just a certain proximity . . . . Love creates that proximity, and the flame jumps from one heart to another heart. There is no question of anybody surrendering, there is no question of anybody believing.

But your question is significant, because even in the East, you will not ordinarily find the master I am defining. The East has fallen deep into darkness. The days of Gautam Buddha are no longer a reality, but just a beautiful memory, a dream that perhaps happened or perhaps somebody dreamt.

One morning a great king, Prasenjita, came to Gautam Buddha. He had in one of his hands a beautiful lotus flower and in the other one of the most precious diamonds of those days. He had come because his wife was persistent, 'When Gautam Buddha is here, you waste your time with idiots, talking about unnecessary things.'

From her very childhood, she had been going to Gautam Buddha; then she got married. Prasenjita had no inclination of that kind but because she was so insistent he said, 'It is worth at least one visit to go and see what kind of man this is.' But he was a man of very great ego, so he took out the most precious diamond from his treasure to present to Gautam Buddha.

He did not want to go there just as an ordinary man. Everybody had to know . . . . In fact, he wanted everybody to know, 'Who is greater—Gautam Buddha or Prasenjita?' That diamond was so precious that many fights and wars had happened over it.

His wife laughed and said, 'You are absolutely unaware of the man I'm taking you to. It is better that you take a flower rather than a stone to present to him.' He could not understand, but he said, 'There is no harm, I can take both. Let us see.'

When he reached there, he offered his diamond, which he was carrying in one of his hands, and Buddha said simply, 'Drop it!' Naturally, what can you do? He dropped it. He thought that perhaps his wife was right. In the other hand, he was carrying the lotus, and as he tried to offer the lotus, Buddha said, 'Drop it!'

He dropped that too, and became a little afraid: the man seemed to be insane, but ten thousand disciples . . . And he stood there, thinking that the people must be thinking he is stupid. And Buddha said the third time, 'Don't you hear me? *Drop it!*' Prasenjita said to himself, 'He is really gone! Now I have dropped the diamond, I have dropped the lotus; now I don't have anything.'

And at that very moment, Sariputta, an old disciple of Gautam Buddha, started laughing. His laughter turned Prasenjita towards him, and he asked him, 'Why are you laughing?'

He said, 'You don't understand the language. He is not saying drop the diamond, he is not saying drop the lotus. He is saying drop yourself, drop the ego. You can have the diamond and you can have the lotus, but drop the ego. Don't take it back.'

Those were beautiful days. Suddenly a new sky opened to Prasenjita. He dropped himself at Gautam Buddha's feet in utter humbleness, and he never left. He became part of the great caravan that used to follow Gautam Buddha. He forgot all about his kingdom, forgot about everything. The only thing that remained was this beautiful man, this tremendous grace, this invisible magnetism, these eyes and this silence. And he was gripped by all this.

It is not a question of belief. It is not a question of conversion, argumentation, it is a question of the highest quality of love.

It is rare to find a master today, and there are many pretenders. One of the things that can be said about the pretenders is that you can recognize them immediately. The moment they ask you to believe in anything, the moment they ask you to follow a certain rule, regulation, the moment they ask you to have faith in them, to never doubt, never question, have indubitable faith—these are the indications of the pretenders. Wherever you find these, escape from the place as fast as you can.

But these people are all over the world, not only in the West but in the East too. It is very rare that you come across a master who gives you dignity, who gives you love, who gives you freedom: who does not create any bondage for you, and who does not make any contract, and who does not want you to be a shadow of him—he wants you to be yourself. The moment you can find a man like this, the greatest moment of your life has arrived. Don't miss it.

Pretenders are many, but authentic masters are immensely rare.

It is unfortunate of our age, of our times, that we have forgotten a certain dimension completely—not only in the West. In the West, they never discovered it, but in the East, we discovered it and lost it. And if there are no more masters who have attained to their ultimate potential, who have become a God unto themselves, then it is very difficult for disciples who are groping in darkness, in blindness, in all kinds of diversions, to find their own dignity, their own self.

My effort here is not to create disciples—that is just the preface—but to create masters, as many masters as possible. The world needs immensely, urgently, many people of awareness, of love, of freedom, of sincerity. Only these people can create a certain spiritual atmosphere that can prevent this world from being destroyed by suicidal forces—which are very powerful, but not more powerful than love.

32

Zorba, the Buddha

What is your notion of rebellion and of a rebel?

MY NOTION ABOUT rebellion and the rebel is very simple: a rebel is a man who does not live like a robot conditioned by the past. Religion, society, culture—anything that is of yesterday does not in any way interfere in his way of life, in his style of life.

He lives individually . . . not as a cog in the wheel, but as an organic unity. His life is not decided by anybody else, but by his own intelligence. The very fragrance of his life is that of freedom. Not only does he live in freedom but he allows everybody else also to live in freedom. He does not allow anybody to interfere in his life nor does he interfere in anybody else's life. To him, life is so sacred—and freedom is the ultimate value—that he can sacrifice everything for it: respectability, status, even life itself.

Freedom, to him, is what God used to be to the so-called religious people in the past. Freedom is his God.

Men have lived down through the ages like sheep, as part of a crowd, following its traditions, conventions, following the old scriptures and old disciplines. But that way of life was anti-individual; if you are a Christian, you cannot be an individual, if you are a Hindu, you cannot be an individual.

A rebel is one who lives totally according to his own light, and risks everything else for his ultimate value of freedom.

The rebel is the contemporary person.

The mobs are not contemporary. Hindus believe in scriptures which are five or ten thousand years old. Such is the case with other religions too; the dead are dominating the living. The rebel rebels against the dead, takes his life in his hands. He is not afraid of being alone; on the contrary, he enjoys his aloneness as one of the most precious treasures. The crowd gives you security, safety— at the cost of your soul. It enslaves you. It gives you guidelines on how to live: what to do, what not to do.

All over the world, every religion has given something like the ten commandments—and these were given by people who had no idea how the future is going to be, how man's consciousness in the future is going to be. It is as if a small child were to write your whole life's story, not knowing what youth means, not knowing what old age means, not knowing what death is.

All religions are primitive, crude—and they have been shaping your life. Naturally, the whole world is full of misery: you are not allowed to be yourself. Every culture wants you to be just a carbon copy, never your original face.

The rebel is one who lives according to his own light, moves according to his own intelligence. He creates his path by walking on it, he does not follow the crowd on the superhighway. His life is dangerous—but a life that is not dangerous is not life at all. He accepts the challenge of the unknown. He does not meet the unknown that is coming in the future, prepared by the past. That creates the whole anguish of humanity; the past prepares you, and the future is never going to be the past. Your yesterday is never going to be your tomorrow.

But up to now, this is how man has lived: your yesterdays prepare you for your tomorrows. The very preparation becomes a hindrance. You cannot breathe freely, you cannot love freely, you cannot dance freely— the past has crippled you in every possible way. The burden of the past is so heavy that everybody is crushed under it. The rebel simply says goodbye to the past.

It is a constant process; hence, to be a rebel means to be continuously in rebellion—because each moment is going to become past; every day is going to become past. It is not that the past is already in the graveyard—you are moving through it every moment. Hence, the rebel has to learn a new art: the art of dying to each moment that has passed, so that he can live freely in the new moment that has come.

A rebel is a continuous process of rebellion; he is not static. And that is where I make a distinction between the revolutionary and the rebel.

The revolutionary is also conditioned by the past. He may not be conditioned by Jesus Christ or Gautam Buddha, but he is conditioned by Karl Marx or Mao Zedong or Joseph Stalin or Adolf Hitler or Benito Mussolini . . . it does not matter who conditions him. The revolutionary has his own holy bible—*Das Kapital*; his holy land—the Soviet Union; his own Mecca—the Kremlin. And just like any other religious person, he is not living according to his own consciousness. He is living according to a conscience created by others. Hence, the revolutionary is nothing but a reactionary. He may be against a certain society, but he is always for another society. He may be against one culture, but he is immediately ready for another culture.

He only goes on moving from one prison into another prison—from Christianity to communism; from one religion to another religion—from Hinduism to Christianity. He changes his prisons.

The rebel simply moves out of the past and never allows the past to dominate him. It is a constant, continuous process. The whole life of the rebel is a fire that burns. To the very last breath, he is fresh, he is young. He will not respond to any situation according to his past experience; he will respond to every situation according to his present consciousness.

To be a rebel, to me, is the only way to be religious, and the so-called religions are not religions at all. They have destroyed humanity completely, enslaved human beings, chained their souls; so, on the surface, it seems that you are free, but deep inside you, religions have created a certain conscience which goes on dominating you. A rebel is one who throws away the whole past because he wants to live his life according to his own longings, according to his own nature—not according to some Gautam Buddha, or according to some Jesus Christ or Moses.

The rebel is the only hope for the future of humanity.

The rebel will destroy all religions, all nations, all races—because they are all rotten, past, hindering the progress of human evolution. They are not allowing anybody to come to his full flowering: they don't want human beings on the earth—they want sheep.

Jesus continuously says, 'I am your shepherd, and you are my sheep . . . .' And I have always wondered that not even a single man stood up and said, 'What kind of nonsense are you talking? If we are sheep, then you are also a sheep; and if you are a shepherd, then we are also shepherds.' Not only his contemporaries . . . but for two thousand years, no Christian has raised the question that it is such an insult to humanity, such a great humiliation to call human beings sheep and to call himself the shepherd, the saviour.

'I have come to save you' . . . and he could not save himself! Still, almost half of humanity is hoping that he will be coming back to save them. You cannot save yourself; the only begotten son of God, Jesus Christ, is needed. And he had promised to his people, 'I will be coming soon, in your own lifetime' . . . and 2,000 years have passed—many lifetimes have passed—and there seems to be no sign, no indication . . . .

But all religions have done the same in different ways. Krishna says in the *Gita* that whenever there is misery, whenever there is anguish, whenever there is the need, 'I will come again and again.' Five thousand years have passed, and he has not been seen even once—never mind 'again and again'! These people, howsoever beautiful their statements may be, were not respectful to humanity.

A rebel respects you, respects life, has a deep reverence for everything that grows, thrives, breathes. He does not put himself above you, holier than you, higher than you; but as just one amongst you. Only one thing he can claim: he is more courageous than you are. He cannot save you, only your courage can save you. He cannot lead you, only your guts can lead you to the fulfilment of your life.

Rebellion is a style of life. To me, it is the only religion which is authentic. Because if you live according to your own light, you may go astray many times, and you may fall many times; but each fall, each going astray will make you wiser, more intelligent, more understanding, more human. There is no other way of learning than by making mistakes. Just don't make the same mistake again. There is no God, except your consciousness. There is no need for any pope, or for Ayatollah Khomeini, or for any *shankaracharya*, to be mediators between you and God. These are the greatest criminals in the world, because they are exploiting your helplessness.

All the priests are pretending that they are mediators between you and the ultimate source of life. They know nothing about it, only you are capable of knowing it. But your source of life is also the ultimate source of life—because we are not separate. No man is an island; we are a vast continent underneath. Perhaps on the surface you look like an island—and there are many islands—but deep down in the ocean, you meet. You are part of one earth, one continent. The same is true about consciousness.

But one has to be free from churches, temples, mosques, synagogues. One has to be just oneself, and take the challenge of life wherever it leads. You are the only guide. You are your own master.

It is an old association and a misunderstanding that to be a nonconformist is to be a rebel. The nonconformist is a reactionary; he acts out of anger, rage, violence and ego. His action is not based on consciousness. Although he goes against society, just to be against society is not necessarily to be right. In fact, most of the time to move from one extreme to another is always to move from one wrong to another wrong.

The rebel is a tremendous balance, and that is not possible without awareness, alertness, and immense compassion. It is not a reaction, it is an action—not against the old, but for the new.

The nonconformist is only against the old, against the established; but he has no creative conception of why he is against it, no vision of the future. What will he do if he succeeds? He will be at a loss, and utterly embarrassed. He has never thought about it. He has not felt the embarrassment because he has never succeeded. His failure has been a great shelter for him.

When I say 'reaction,' I mean your orientation is basically dependent: you are not acting out of freedom and independence. It has very deep implications. It means your action is just a by-product; it also means that your action can be controlled very easily.

There is a small story about Mulla Nasruddin. He was a nonconformist, a fundamental reactionary, an absolutely negative mind.

If his father said, 'You have to go to the right,' you could be certain he would go to the left. Soon the father became aware of this, and then there was no problem. When he wanted him to go to the right, he would say, 'Please go to the left,' and Mulla would go to the right. He was disobeying, he was a nonconformist, but he was completely unaware that he was being dictated to, ordered, controlled and doing actually what his father wanted him to do.

Slowly, slowly, he became aware—'What is the matter? Before, my father used to be very angry that he had told me to go right and I went left. I am continuing to be as disobedient as ever, but now he never complains.' Soon, he figured out the strategy.

One day, the old father and Nasruddin were crossing the river with their donkey, and on the donkey was a big bag of sugar. The bag was leaning more towards the right, and there was a danger that it might slip and fall into the river.

The father was behind and he knew, 'If I say, "Move the bag towards the left," I have got such a strange son that he will move it immediately towards the right, and the bag will fall into the river and all the sugar will be lost.' So he shouted, 'Nasruddin, move the bag towards the right,' hoping that he was going to move it to the left according to the old experience.

But by this time Nasruddin had figured it out. He said, 'Okay,' and moved the bag towards the right and the bag fell into the river!

The father said, 'What happened, are you no longer disobedient?'

He said, 'Now I will decide each time whether to be obedient or not. I will not have a fixed philosophy but I will move according to the situation—because you have been cunning with me, you have been cheating me. I'm your son and still you have been cheating me! You have been ordering me in such a way that I should disobey. From today onwards, be alert—I may obey, I may not. I am not going to be predictable, controllable, in your hands anymore.'

The nonconformist is always in the hands of society and the establishment. The establishment just has to be a little more clever and cunning, and then he can use the nonconformist very easily, without any difficulty.

But the establishment can never use the rebel because he is not reacting to the establishment. He has a vision of the future, of a new man, of a new humanity. He is working to create that dream, to transform it into reality. If he is against society, he is against it because society is a hindrance to his dream. His focus is not on the establishment but on an unknown future, a potential possibility. He acts out of his freedom, out of his vision, out of his dream. His consciousness decides which way to go.

✳

How is your rebel concerned with Zorba, the Buddha?

My rebel, my new man, is Zorba, the Buddha.

Mankind has lived believing either in the reality of the soul and the illusoriness of matter, or in the reality of matter and the illusoriness of the soul.

You can divide the humanity of the past into spiritualists and materialists. But nobody has bothered to look at the reality of man. He is both together. He is neither just spirituality—he is not just consciousness—nor is he merely matter. He is a tremendous harmony between matter and consciousness.

Or perhaps matter and consciousness are not two things, but only two aspects of one reality: matter is the outside of consciousness, and consciousness is the interiority of matter. But there has not been a single philosopher, sage, or religious mystic in the past who has declared this unity; they were all in favour of dividing man, calling one side real and the other side unreal. This has created an atmosphere of schizophrenia all over the earth.

You cannot live just as a body. That's what Jesus means when he says, 'Man cannot live by bread alone'— but this is only half the truth. You cannot live just as consciousness alone, you cannot live without bread either. You have two dimensions of your being, and both the dimensions have to be fulfilled, given equal opportunity for growth. But the past has been either in favour of one and against the other, or in favour of the other and against the first one.

Man as a totality has not been accepted. This has created misery, anguish, and a tremendous darkness; a night that has lasted for thousands of years, that seems to have no end. If you listen to the body, you condemn yourself; if you don't listen to the body, you suffer—you are hungry, you are poor, you are thirsty. If you listen only to consciousness, your growth will be lopsided: your consciousness will grow but your body will shrink, and the balance will be lost. And in the balance is your health, your wholeness, your joy, your song, your dance.

The West has chosen to listen to the body, and has become completely deaf as far as the reality of consciousness is concerned. The ultimate result is great science, great technology, an affluent society, a richness of things mundane, worldly. And amidst all this abundance, a poor man without a soul, completely lost—not knowing who he is, not knowing why he is, feeling almost an accident or a freak of nature. Unless consciousness grows with the richness of the material world, the body—matter—becomes too heavy and the soul becomes too weak. You are too burdened by your own inventions, your own discoveries. Rather than creating a beautiful life for you, they create a life which is felt by all the intelligentsia of the West as not worth living.

The East has chosen consciousness and has condemned matter and everything material, the body included, as *maya*, as illusory, as a mirage in a desert which only appears but has no reality in itself. The East has created a Gautam Buddha, a Mahavira, a Patanjali, a Kabir, a Farid, a Raidas—a long line of people with great consciousness, with great awareness. But it has also created millions of poor people, hungry, starving, dying like dogs—with not enough food, no pure water to drink, not enough clothes, not enough shelters.

A strange situation . . . . In the West, every six months, they have to sink billions and billions of dollars' worth of milk products and other foodstuff in the ocean, because it is surplus. They don't want to overload their warehouses, they don't want to lower their prices and destroy their economic structure. On the one hand, in Ethiopia, one thousand people were dying every day and, at the same time, the European Common Market was destroying so

much food that the cost of destroying it was millions of
dollars. That is not the cost of the food; it is the cost
of taking it to the ocean, and throwing it into the ocean.
Who is responsible for this situation?

The richest man in the West is searching for his soul
and finding himself hollow, without any love, only lust;
without any prayer, only parrot-like words that he has
been taught in the Sunday schools. He has no religiousness,
no feeling for other human beings, no reverence for life,
birds, trees, animals—destruction is so easy.

Hiroshima and Nagasaki would not have happened if
man were not thought to be just matter. So many nuclear
weapons would not have been piled up if man had been
thought to be a hidden God, a hidden splendour; not to be
destroyed but to be discovered, not to be destroyed but to
be brought into the light—a temple of God. But if man is
just matter, just chemistry, physics, a skeleton covered
with skin, then with death everything dies, nothing remains.
That's why it becomes possible for an Adolf Hitler to kill
six million people, without a hitch. If all people are just
matter, there is no question of even thinking twice.

The West has lost its soul, its interiority. Surrounded
by meaninglessness, boredom, anguish, it is not finding
itself. All the success of science is proving of no use
because the house is full of everything, but the master of
the house is missing. Here, in the East, the master is alive
but the house is empty. It is difficult to rejoice with hungry
stomachs, with sick bodies, with death surrounding you; it
is impossible to meditate. So, unnecessarily, we have been
losers. All our saints, philosophers, spiritualists and
materialists are responsible for this immense crime against
man.

Zorba, the Buddha is the answer. It is the synthesis of
matter and soul. It is a declaration that there is no conflict

between matter and consciousness, that we can be rich on both sides. We can have everything that the world can provide, that science and technology can produce, and we can still have everything that a Buddha, a Kabir, a Nanak finds in his inner being—the flowers of ecstasy, the fragrance of godliness, the wings of ultimate freedom.

Zorba, the Buddha is the new man, is the rebel.

His rebellion consists of destroying the schizophrenia of man, destroying the dividedness—destroying spirituality as against materialism, and destroying materialism as against spirituality. It is a manifesto that body and soul are together: that existence is full of spirituality, that even mountains are alive, that even trees are sensitive, that the whole existence is both—or perhaps just one energy expressing itself in two ways, as matter and as consciousness. When energy is purified, it expresses itself as consciousness; when energy is crude, unpurified, dense, it appears as matter. But the whole existence is nothing but an energy field.

This is my experience, it is not my philosophy. And this is supported by modern physics and its researches: existence is energy.

We can allow man to have both worlds together. He need not renounce this world to get the other world, nor has he to deny the other world to enjoy this world. In fact, to have only one world while you are capable of having both is to be unnecessarily poor.

Zorba, the Buddha is the richest possibility. He will live his nature to its utmost and will sing songs of this earth. He will not betray the earth, and he will not betray the sky either. He will claim all that this earth has—all flowers, all pleasures—and he will also claim all stars of the sky. He will claim the whole existence as his home.

The man of the past was poor because he divided

existence. The new man, my rebel, Zorba, the Buddha, claims the whole world as his home. All that it contains is for us, and we have to use it in every possible way— without any guilt, without any conflict, without any choice. Choicelessly enjoy all that matter is capable of, and rejoice in all that consciousness is capable of.

Be a Zorba, but don't stop there. Go on moving towards being a Buddha. Zorba is half, Buddha is half.

There is an ancient story:

In a forest near a city there lived two beggars. They were enemies, as all professionals are—two doctors, two professors, two saints. One was blind and the other was lame, and both were very competitive; the whole day, they were competing with each other in the city.

But one night their huts caught fire, because the whole forest was on fire. The blind man could run out, but he could not see *where* to run, he could not see where the fire had not yet spread. The lame man could see that there were still possibilities of getting out of this fire, but he could not run out. The fire was too fast, too wild, so the lame man could only see his death coming.

They realized that they needed each other. The lame man had a sudden realization, 'The other man can run, the blind man can run, and I can see.' They forgot all their competition. In such a critical moment, when both were facing death, each necessarily forgot all stupid enmities. They created a great synthesis; they agreed that the blind man would carry the lame man on his shoulders, and they would function as one man—the lame man could see, and the blind man could run. They saved their lives. And because they saved each other's lives, they became friends; for the first time they dropped their antagonism.

Zorba is blind—he cannot see, but he can dance, he

can sing, he can rejoice. The Buddha can see, but he can only see. He is pure eyes, just clarity and perception, but he cannot dance; he is crippled, he cannot sing, he cannot rejoice.

It is time. The world is a wildfire; everybody's life is in danger. The meeting of Zorba and Buddha can save the whole humanity. Their meeting is the only hope. Buddha can contribute consciousness, clarity, eyes to see beyond, eyes to see that which is almost invisible. Zorba can give his whole being to Buddha's vision and let it not remain just a dry vision, but make it a dancing, rejoicing, ecstatic way of life.

I am giving Buddha energy to dance, and I am giving Zorba eyes to see beyond the skies to faraway destinies of existence and evolution. My rebel is nobody other than Zorba, the Buddha.

Osho Commune International

An Invitation To Experience

OSHO COMMUNE INTERNATIONAL is a unique experiment: an opportunity for individuals to experience a radical approach to meditation and silence. This is the place for the evolution of Zorba the Buddha, someone whose feet can dance on the ground and whose hands can touch the stars. An environment beyond nations, races and religions—where the international language is laughter and silence. A place to be alone together, where each can learn from the other while respecting everyone's unique individuality.

As Osho describes it, 'The very air has a different vibe: even when you go away, your song, your dance, your joy go on vibrating here.'

Now Osho Commune International has evolved into the world's largest centre for meditation and spiritual growth, and offers hundreds of different methods for exploring and experiencing the inner world.

Every year, thousands of seekers from all over the world come to celebrate and meditate together in Osho's Buddhafield. The commune grounds are full of lush green gardens, pools and waterfalls, elegant snow-white swans and colourful peacocks, as well as beautiful buildings and pyramids. Such a peaceful and harmonious atmosphere makes it very easy to experience the inner silence in a joyful way.

(i) For detailed information to participate in this Buddhafield contact:

Osho Commune International
17 Koregaon Park, Pune-411001, MS, India
Ph: 020 4019999 Fax: 020 4019990
Email: visitor@osho.net Website: www.osho.com

(ii) Further Information
Many of Osho's books have been translated and published in a variety of languages worldwide.

For information about Osho, his meditations, and the address of an Osho meditation/information centre near you, contact:

Osho Commune International
17 Koregaon Park, Pune-411001, MS, India
Ph: 020 4019999 Fax: 020 4019990
Email: visitor@osho.net Website: www.osho.com

For information about Osho's books and tapes contact:

Sadhana Foundation
17 Koregaon Park, Pune-411001, MS, India
Ph: 020 4019999 Fax: 020 4019990
Email: distrib@osho.net Website: www.osho.com

www.osho.com
A comprehensive website in different languages featuring Osho's meditations, books and tapes, an outline tour of Osho Commune International, a list of Osho Information Centres worldwide, and a selection of Osho's talks.